Walk!

The Brecon Beacons

with

Bob Greaves

DISCOVERY WALKING GUIDES LTD

Walk! The Brecon Beacons
First Edition - January 2006
Reprinted April 2009 with correction to Walk 15 to
follow official 'Rights of Way'.
Reprinted May 2012
Copyright © 2006, 2009, 2012

Published by
Discovery Walking Guides Ltd
10 Tennyson Close, Northampton NN5 7HJ, England

Mapping supplied by **Global Mapping Limited**
(www.globalmapping.com)

Mapping sourced from | OS Ordnance Survey   This product includes mapping
data licensed from **Ordnance Survey®** with the
permission of the Controller of Her Majesty's
Stationery Office. © Crown Copyright 2005. All
rights reserved.
Licence Number 40044851

Photographs
All photographs in this book are the property of the
author; the majority were taken by the author; others by
Sally Mae, and Moth.

Front Cover Photographs

| **Taking a rest during the ascent of Corn Du (Walk 27)** | **Just after the bridge at Wp.8 (Walk 10)** |

| **Carreg Cennen Castle (Walk 40)** | **Usk Reservoir (Walk 38)** |

ISBN 9781904946175
Text and photographs* © Bob Greaves

Walk!
The Brecon Beacons

CONTENTS

THE WALKS

THE AUTHOR

Educated at a traditional grammar school, Bob Greaves had to choose, aged thirteen, between the 'Science' and 'Arts' sides. As he was good at sums he chose the 'Science' side and went on to a degree in Pure Mathematics and a career in the computer industry.

Introduced to walking and maps as a child, he has found his way independently to many parts of Britain and walked in Ireland, France, Austria, Czech Republic, Greece, Madeira (a favourite) as well as La Gomera and La Palma in the Canaries. As a walk leader, he has delighted in designing a variety of itineraries that meet the demands of different groups.

Now, with two married daughters and six grandchildren under his belt, so to speak, he has grasped the opportunity to combine his passion with his computer experience to embark on a new career researching and writing walking books.

ACKNOWLEDGEMENTS

Many thanks must go to Ros and David Brawn, firstly for trusting me sufficiently to embark on this enterprise, secondly for being extremely supportive when mid-project I became seriously ill but mainly for their sensitivity in giving me just the right form of encouragement at every stage. Thank you both. I'd also like to thank Moth for accompanying me during two days of early research in gloriously hot weather; a result being her back featuring on the front cover, Rob, for his continued interest, and Jo, for her positive feedback on reading early drafts. But greatest thanks must go to Sally Mae, my proof-reader, sometime camera wielder and encourager of my "bits of whimsy". Her support is epitomised by her insistence on standing intrepidly on the 'diving board' at the top of **Fan y Big** (Walk 28) to have her photograph taken despite the whole area being infested with flying ants!

Usk Reservoir

There are forty great walks here, ranging from a gentle stroll around **Usk Reservoir** (Walk 38) to, in **Grwynne Fawr** (Walk 19), a challenging four peaks in a day.

My aim throughout is to inspire confidence. Perhaps you've only ventured out on walks with a group, concerned that you might get lost, you need have no such fears with this book and a GPS.

Pen Allt-mawr, on Walk 19

I've tackled each one of these walks in the last year and a half and the routes shown on the maps are the precise routes I took, recorded on a GPS - for those without a GPS, each walk includes detailed route descriptions and the grid coordinates of every waypoint.

BRECON BEACONS NATIONAL PARK

Carmarthen Fan

Fan Foel

All the walks are within the National Park, an area of great beauty and tremendous variety.

Lower Neuadd Reservoir

High peaks hide glacial lakes in ancient moorland; man-made reservoirs and canals now blend with their natural surroundings, while waterfalls cascade down secret gorges and canals.

Castles, churches and monasteries bear witness to the rich history and heritage that can be absorbed on the walks..

Cerreg Cennen Castle

Monmouthshire and Brecon Canal

The area is bounded by the towns of **Abergavenny**, **Hay-on Wye**, **Brecon**, **Llandovery**, **Llandeilo** and **Merthyr Tydfil** and consist of four distinct areas which, running from east to west, are **The Black Mountains**, **Brecon Beacons**, **Fforest Fawr** and **The Black Mountain**.

Cwmyoy Church

Confusing - but explained by **The Black Mountains** being the apt English name for the series of ridges and valleys to the east and **Y Mynydd Du** (translated as 'The Black Mountain' in English) being the equally appropriate Welsh name for the isolated area of moorland to the west.

Llanthony Priory

The National Park Visitor Centre at **Libanus**, six miles south west of **Brecon** on the A470 is well worth a visit, not just as a comprehensive source of information on all that can be enjoyed in the park, but also for its award winning tea room with outstanding views.

WHERE TO STAY

For a wide choice of accommodation visit www.visitbreconbeacons.com but, for what it's worth, I have personal experience of several places, detailed in the appendices at the back of this book.

HISTORY

Iron age forts were built from around 600 BC to enclose communities and their livestock when under attack. There are twenty or so of these in the National Park, the most well-known, due to their prominent positioning and level of preservation, being **Carn Goch** (Walk 39), **Crug Hywel** (Walks 18 and 19) and **Castell Dinas** (Walk 20).

The Romans struggled to set up civilian settlements in the **Brecon Beacons**, leaving the legacy of a road system linking a network of fortified camps, the best preserved being **Y Gaer**, in farmland just west of **Brecon** itself. The Normans also failed to impose their influence though the triangle of castles at **Skenfrith**, **Grosmont** and **Llantilio Crossenny** to the east and the stronghold of **Brecon** itself demonstrate their strength in the valleys.

The area largely avoided the frenetic industrial growth of coal and iron in the **South Wales** valleys, but there are some examples of major industrial endeavour such as at **Garn-Ddyrys** (Walk 13). Ironically, these were the reason for the development of the **Brecknock and Abergavenny Canal**, now a tranquil, scenic haven (Walks 22 and 23).

Brecknock and Abergavenny Canal - a tranquil, scenic haven

GEOLOGY

Old Red Sandstone makes up most of the National Park and produces the thick, red, sticky concoction often taken home on boots. Its easily weathered consistency produces the rounded outlines which, below wide blue skies, are so attractive.

Corn Du from Fan Fawr

Llyn y Fan Fawr

Llyn Cwm Llwch (Walks 25 and 27) and **Llyn y Fan Fawr** (Walk 35) are classic examples of glacial lakes, scooped out by ice but left when glaciers retreated and from the ridges above them text book views of *cwms* and U-shaped valleys abound.

However, along the southern boundary of the National Park the sandstone changes to limestone with bands of millstone grit, thus creating a magical land of wooded gorges, waterfalls, caves and potholes where the **Mellte**, **Hepste** and **Nedd** tumble down to form the river **Neath** at **Pontneddfechan** (Walks 33 and 34).

Sgwd Ddwli

WEATHER

One advantage of walking with a GPS is that the dire warnings of the mists coming down don't have to be disturbing us. Nevertheless, it is true that the weather can change very rapidly and it's not much fun walking in the cold and damp of a cloud with five metre visibility. I've learned to trust the information to be found at:

www.metoffice.gov.uk/outdoor/mountainsafety/brecon.html

- so much so that on several occasions I've started climbing towards peaks enshrouded in cloud, confident that by midday they would be clear.

THE ROUTES

The numerical order of the walks is generally east to west. Each of the routes consist of a summary, some key information, how to get to the start by car followed by a detailed description.

The walking speeds given in each walk are those that I actually did, minus any breaks. Obviously you're likely to walk faster or slower than me, so I suggest you walk a couple of the easier, shorter routes first and see how your times compare with mine so that you can factor that in. The vertigo risk is very conservative; most walkers won't have problems with any of the walks.

The access by car directions start from **Abergavenny**, **Hay-on-Wye**, **Brecon** or the major roundabout just north of **Merthyr Tydfil**. I've included how to get there details of the walks where the start is accessible by public transport in Appendix B.

You may have twigged by the presence of a single author's name on the front cover that the chatty 'we' style is a literary style introduced by Ros and David Brawn in the first Walk! book. The intention is to include the reader/walker with the author. It was a fun way of writing.

A NOTE ABOUT SPELLING

Many places have both English and Welsh names, I have gone along with the Ordnance Survey ruling even where this seems to run contra to the norm, for example **Ysgyryd Fawr** rather than 'Skirrid Fawr'. See Appendix A for an explanation of some of the elements of Welsh place names.

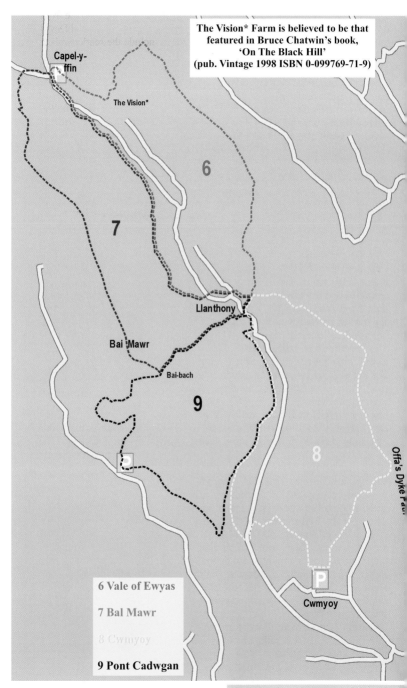

The Vision* Farm is believed to be that
featured in Bruce Chatwin's book,
'On The Black Hill'
(pub. Vintage 1998 ISBN 0-099769-71-9)

Capel-y-ffin

The Vision*

6

7

Llanthony

Bai Mawr

Bai-bach

9

8

Offa's Dyke Path

Cwmyoy

6 Vale of Ewyas

7 Bal Mawr

8 Cwmyoy

9 Pont Cadwgan

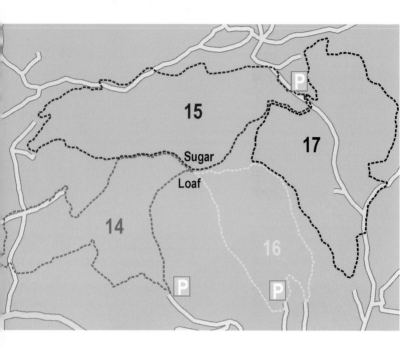

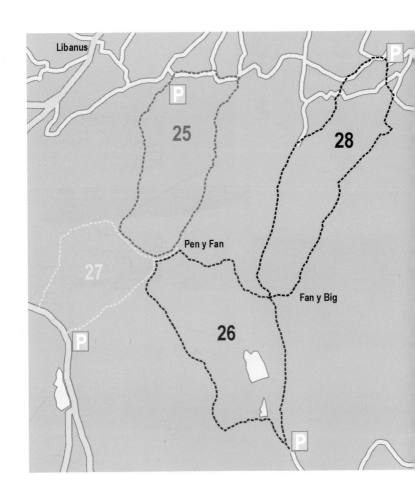

Libanus

25

28

27

Pen y Fan

Fan y Big

26

25 Pen y Fan from Cwm Llwch

26 Pen y Fan from Taf Fechan

27 Pen y Fan from Pont ar Daf

28 Fan y Big

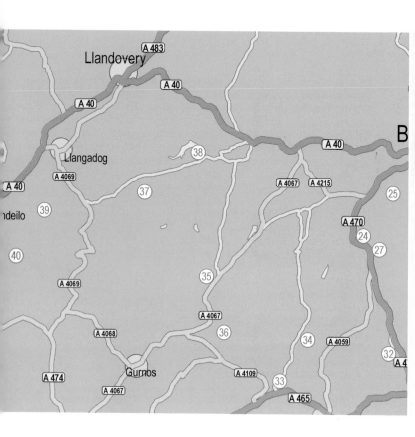

GPS ANOMALIES

Contrary to myth, perhaps spread by the anti-GPS brigade, in a year's research for this book we found no deterioration of GPS performance in adverse weather conditions - including a snowstorm! The places we did have a problem were where dense trees, particularly conifers, completely covered our way and in wooded canyons. Therefore unsurprisingly, the waterfall walks were the most affected.

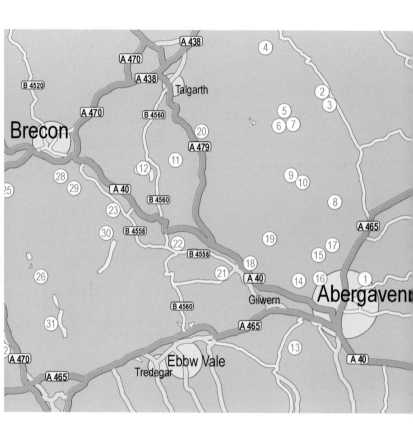

In detail, routes affected are:-

The only area where this can make routes difficult to follow is between Wps.3&9 on Walks 33&34, which both cover the stretch between the footbridge over **Afon Mellte** above **Sgwd Clun-gwyn** and **Sgwd yr Eira** itself. However, as this is a tourist area with **Sgwd yr Eira** well signposted, even if the exact route isn't followed, the circular walks can be successfully completed without difficulty.

3 our rating for effort/exertion:-
1 very easy **2** easy **3** average
4 energetic **5** strenuous

 approximate **time** to complete
a walk (compare your times
against ours early in a walk) -
does not include stopping time

 5 miles/8km approximate walking
distance in
miles/kilometres

 250m approximate
ascents/descents in
850m metres (N=negligible)

 circular route  **linear** route **figure of eight** route risk of **vertigo**

 3 **refreshments** (may be at start or end of a route only)

- Walk descriptions include:
- timing in minutes, shown as (40M)
- compass directions, shown as (NW)
- heights in metres, shown as (1355m)
- GPS waypoints, shown as (Wp.3)

Notes on the text
Place names are shown in **bold text**,
except where we refer to a written
sign, when they are enclosed in single
quotation marks. Local or unusual
words are shown in *italics*, and are
explained in the accompanying text.

ORDNANCE SURVEY MAPPING

All the map sections which accompany the detailed walk descriptions in
Walk! The Brecon Beacons are reproduced under Ordnance Survey licence
from the digital versions of the latest Explorer 1:25,000 scale maps. Each map
section is then re-scaled to the 40,000 scale used in DWG's Walk!/Walks
series of guide books. Walking Route and GPS Waypoints are then drawn onto
the map section to produce the map illustrating the detailed walk description.

Walk! The Brecon Beacons map sections are sufficient for following the
detailed walk descriptions, but for planning your adventures in this region we
strongly recommend that you purchase the latest OS Explorer maps.

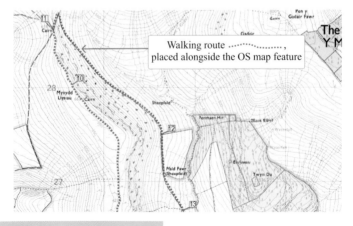

Walking route ·······················,
placed alongside the OS map feature

The GPS Waypoint lists provided in this book are as recorded by Bob Greaves while researching the detailed walk descriptions. Waypoint symbols are numbered so that they can be directly identified with the walk description and waypoint list. All GPS Waypoints are subject to the accuracy of GPS units in the particular location of each waypoint.

In the dramatic landscapes of the Brecon Beacons, GPS reception is surprisingly good for the majority of Bob's walking routes; see Bob's waypoint notes on pages 16-17.

Satellite Reception
Accurate location fixes for your GPS unit depend upon you receiving signals from four or more satellites. Providing you have good batteries, and that you wait until your GPS has full 'satellite acquisition' before starting out, your GPS will perform well in the Brecon Beacons. Where Bob has encountered poor satellite reception it is mentioned in the walk description.

Manually Inputting Waypoints
GPS Waypoints are quoted for the OSGB (Ordnance Survey Great Britain) datum and BNG (British National Grid) coordinates, making them identical with the OS grid coordinates of the position they refer to. To manually input the Waypoints into your GPS we suggest that you:

- switch on your GPS and select 'simulator/standby' mode
- check that your GPS is set to the OSGB datum and BNG 'location/position format'
- input the GPS Waypoints into a 'route' with the same number as the walking route; then when you call up the 'route' in the Brecon Beacons there will be no confusion as to which walking route it refers
- repeat the inputting of waypoints into routes until you have covered all the routes you plan to walk, or until you have used up the memory capacity of your GPS
- turn off your GPS. When you turn your GPS back on it should return to its normal navigation mode.

Note that GPS Waypoints complement the routes in Walk! The Brecon Beacons, and are not intended as an alternative to the detailed walking route descriptions.

Personal Navigator Files (PNFs) CD version 3.01
Edited versions of Bob's original GPS research tracks and waypoints are available as downloadable files on our PNFs CD, which also includes all the edited GPS tracks and waypoints for all the Walk!/Walks guide books published by DWG along with GPS Utility Special edition software. See DWG websites for more information:

www.walking.demon.co.uk & www.dwgwalking.co.uk

GPS The Easy Way (£4.99)
If you are confused by talk of GPS, but are interested in how this modern navigational aid could enhance your walking enjoyment, then simply seek out a copy of GPS The Easy Way, the UK's best selling GPS manual.

WALKING EQUIPMENT

Most importantly, walk with what you're comfortable in. What follows are simply some of my personal thoughts.

- Feet must be comfortable - I usually wear **boots, lightweight but waterproof**, and **two pairs of socks**. But when it's hot I love to walk in sandals which have much improved recently; those with toe guards are a boon.

- **Rucksack** - as small and lightweight as I can get away with, the only other condition being that it must be waterproof, getting a pullover out of a plastic bag when freezing in a gale is not an option.

- Sunstroke - even when it's cloudy I wear a **hat** during the summer, though I have to admit it's more crucial if you have a bald spot on top!

- Dehydration - not taking **enough water** is a temptation because it is so heavy. I drink plenty before setting out then little and often, remembering that feeling thirsty is the body's way of saying that you're beginning to dehydrate. Making water easily available helps, the method by which a tube hangs permanently in front of your face from a pouch in the top of your rucksack may look naff but works well.

- Energy - in addition to my lunchtime **sandwiches** I take **chocolate, nuts** and **dried fruit** which, in addition to supplying an energy boost, make me popular with companions.

- Rain - I have **waterproof, lightweight, breathable tops and bottoms**, the important lesson is to put them on at the slightest indication of precipitation rather than delay because it might stop in the next five minutes.

- Altitude - It gets much colder higher up, if it's a warm day I'll just wear a **T-shirt**, if cooler a **shirt** and a **fleece**. Either way, I pack a warm **pullover, gloves** and a **woolly hat** that I can pull down over my ears.

- **GPS** with **spare batteries**.

- Emergencies - Take a **loud whistle**, the internationally recognized distress signal is six long blasts in quick succession at one minute intervals. Don't expect to be able to get a mobile signal in an emergency.

- Other things - **Plasters, mozzie cream, suncream, tissues**.

1 YSGYRYD FAWR

Also known as **Skirrid Fawr** and **The Holy Mountain**, this is the first elevation encountered when approaching the Brecon Beacons from the east. This route serves as an ideal introduction as it is relatively short and easy, but affords views right round from **Blorenge** (Route 13) in the south west to **Hay Bluff** (Route 4) in the north west encompassing **Sugar Loaf** (Routes 14,15 and 16), **Bryn Arw** (Route 17) and **The Black Mountains** (Routes 2,3,5,6,7,8 and 9) on the way.

We start by following the well-trodden path to the summit, but eschew returning the same way as most walkers seem to do, descending the eastern flank and rounding the base of the northern end before returning through the woods to the car park.

*none on the route, but there are several pubs along the road between **Abergavenny** and **Skenfrith**.

Access by car:

Coming from **Abergavenny**, we take the B4521 toward **Ross on Wye**. There is a layby on the left after 3 miles with a 'Ysgyryd Fawr' National Trust sign. If you reach the **Walnut Tree Inn**, nationally renowned for its cuisine, you've gone too far.

We start off (Wp.1 0M), passing between the National Trust sign and a padlocked gate, down a grey chippings track - not the most comfortable walking surface. This soon turns right (NW), and we are presented with what looks like an exercise in perspective as the track runs dead straight between green hedges which rise gently ahead. The chippings end when we reach double gates with a stile to the left, and our track now winds right and left before we turn right (Wp.2 6M N) onto a woodland path by a yellow waymark.

This well-trodden path climbs more steeply, with occasional steps aiding our ascent. We cross two tracks and after the second (Wp.3 8M) there is another yellow waymark and we continue upward to reach a gate (Wp.4 14m). Through the gate, we take the right hand path (NE) to continue climbing. Our path is sometimes neatly reinforced with stones, a reminder that the path was used for centuries past to reach the chapel on the summit. We emerge from the wood (Wp.5 20M) to a magnificent view to the right, a good place for a breather - most of the work is done!

Here, the path splits in two. Either will do, as the left fork path has been made by those impatient to reach the ridge with its wonderful views to east and west but we continue on the right path (NNE) proceeding more gently up the eastern flank to the ridge (Wp.6 23M), the way ahead well defined. We pass a large rock on the left carved with initials and names

We make the ridge

The summit at 40 minutes

(Wp.7 30M), and eventually reach the summit (Wp.8 40M) where the gateposts and a depression in the ground just before we reach the trig point, are all that remain of the chapel.

Several steep paths with loose stones lead straight down from the summit but are too exciting to recommend as a route! Instead we retrace our steps (SSW) for 150 metres and, by a depression, (Wp.9 45M) take a path on the left (NE) which takes us nearly back on ourselves. This is not too obvious, particularly if walked when the bracken is high. Once we've found it, the path is reasonably distinct though nothing like as well-used as our route up and takes us down, not too steeply.

Towards the bottom of the hill, the bracken ends and the route is not so obvious but we continue in the same direction towards a wire fence with a rough track in front of it. On reaching the track (Wp.10 53M), we turn left (N) onto it. The track goes through a gate, but we make our way around the base of the hill, towards a prominent post, possibly once a signpost. From this post (Wp.11 55M) we follow the path ahead (W) with the 'exciting' precipitous descent from the summit on our left. We encounter two small streams that run off the hill but they can be negotiated without getting wet, thanks to well positioned stepping stones. Our route keeps turning left (SW) for us to approach a gully (Wp.12 61M) that runs between **Ysgyryd Fawr** and a smaller hill.

The path now passes through woodland, with occasional views of the **Black Mountains** from between the trees. Proceeding gently downhill and meeting a mossy drystone wall on our right (SE), we find ourselves back at the gate we encountered earlier (Wp.4 85M). Going through the gate we retrace our steps down the hill, back down the grey chippings to the layby (Wp.1 96M).

2 CRIB Y GARTH

This route climbs steadily up the **Olchon Valley** and returns along the narrow, most easterly, of the **Black Mountain** ridges which is popularly known as **The Cat's Back**. Although quite compact, it still allows us a chance to experience some really wild moorland. Most walkers are tempted straight up onto the ridge from the car park, but we do the walk in reverse which provides us with stunning views when returning along the ridge, not only to left and right but also forward down into the **Longtown** valley.

3   2 H   4.5 miles/7km   300m / 300m   0

Access by car:

Coming from **Abergavenny**, we take the A465 towards **Hereford**. After 6 miles and just after the village of **Pandy**, we turn left and follow signs to **Longtown**. After passing through the village we take the second left turn signed **Little Black Hill**. This narrow lane runs between high hedges and soon we see the vista of **Crib y Garth** rising directly in front of us. Turning right by a signpost to a picnic site, we climb steeply to the small car park/picnic site at the end of the lane.

> **Longer Version**
>
> A longer version can be made by starting on the **Hatterrall Ridge** walk (Route 3) and joining this route at the cairn (Wp.8).

The ridge tempts us

Starting from the car park (Wp.1 0M) we resist the temptation of the immediate ascent to the ridge and walk back down the lane (SSE) the way we've just come in the car. At the T junction (Wp.2 6M) we turn right (NW) and wander along a quiet lane often overhung with foliage from both sides which creates a green tunnel.

After 700 metres (Wp.3 28M) we take a track that forks to the right and rises gently, and soon go through a wooden gate (Wp.4 32M) into a field and the track becomes slightly sunken with a bank to the left, which in winter can become very muddy. There are several parallel paths which have been made in the field up to our right by those who've gone before us.

Passing out of the field through a metal gate (Wp.5 37M), our way is now a well-defined path which climbs more steeply, crossing innumerable streams. The largest of these has created a gully into which we drop down (Wp.6 40M). Climbing out the other side, the bank to our right is covered with heather and bilberries, and to our left is a ravine where the water of the **Olchon Brook** crashes over rocks. Eventually, the going flattens out (Wp.7 60M) and we ignore smaller paths to left and right until we reach a small cairn at a T-junction (Wp.8 69M).

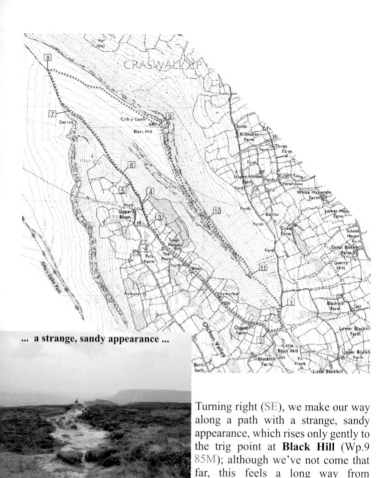

... a strange, sandy appearance ...

Turning right (SE), we make our way along a path with a strange, sandy appearance, which rises only gently to the trig point at **Black Hill** (Wp.9 85M); although we've not come that far, this feels a long way from civilisation.

We are drawn down onto the ridge ahead which quickly narrows and becomes increasingly rocky so that we have to be careful where we put our feet. The view is fantastic at any time, but is at its best when the sun begins to go down. Stop to make the best of it! Half way along (Wp.10 101M), the remnants of some old quarrying can provide a useful shelter if the wind gets up, which can happen here quite suddenly.

At the end of the ridge (Wp.11 112M), we drop down steeply to cross a stile and arrive back at the car park (Wp.1 119M).

Half way along the ridge

3 HATTERRALL RIDGE

Our route starts from the same car park as **Walk 2 Crib y Garth** but crosses the **Olchon Valley** and climbs steeply up to traverse the northern end of **Hatterrall Ridge**, almost to **Hay Bluff**, before returning down the valley. It includes part of **Offa's Dyke**, the long distance footpath that runs between **Chepstow** and **Prestatyn** broadly following the ancient earthwork built in the eighth century to defend England from the marauding Welsh. **Capel-y-ffin** (Route 5), **Vale of Ewyas** (Route 6) and **Cwmyoy** (Route 8) also include parts of **Offa's Dyke**, demonstrating its overwhelming significance to the area.

An even more satisfying, longer version can be made by combining the route with **Walk 2 Crib y Garth**. Instead of returning down the **Olchon Valley**, continue straight on at the small cairn (Wp. 11) and follow Route 2 over **Black Hill** to the car park.

4 | 3H 40M | 8.5 miles/13.6km | 450m 450m | 0

Access by car:
Coming from **Abergavenny**, we take the A465 towards **Hereford**. After six miles and just after the village of **Pandy**, we turn left and follow signs to **Longtown**. After passing through the village we take the second left turn signed 'Little Black Hill'. This narrow lane runs between high hedges and soon we see the vista of **Crib y Garth** rising directly in front of us. At a fork, we take the right hand option, then turning right by a signpost to a picnic site, we climb steeply to the small car park/picnic site at the end of the lane.

From the car park (Wp.1 0M), we return the way we've just driven (S), regretting the steep downhill because we know we'll have to struggle uphill sometime later to compensate. Turning left at the bottom of the hill (SE), we pass a metal barred gate on our right and, immediately afterwards, look for a wooden signpost on the same side (Wp.2 5M) which is not obvious as it merges with the woodland behind it. Plunging into the woods (SW), we are gratified to see a yellow waymark which confirms our way down through the scrubby woodland. After a waymarked stile, we cross a muddy track (W) to go through a narrow wooden gate and down beside **Black Hill Farm** (undergoing renovation). Another stile brings us to a track running down the other side of the farm and we notice a superior tree house with a glass window.

Not obvious but for another yellow waymark, we follow the path that is directly across the track down the right hand side of a little gorge with a stream running in it. Beautiful views of our objective, the **Hatterrall Ridge** confront us before we reach a footbridge (Wp.3 20M) which crosses the river that gives its name to the **Olchon Valley**.

The Hatterrall Ridge

A sign tells us that the footpath has been diverted and we follow more yellow waymarks to go up between a gorge made by another stream and a molehill beleaguered field. Crossing a wooden stile to the right of a black gate (Wp.4 25M), we turn left (S) into an attractive sunken lane with trees meeting overhead but before we've really enjoyed the experience to the full turn right (SW) into another lane. This climbs steeply directly towards **Hatterrall Ridge** which looks quite a challenge from here. After the lane turns sharply left, we find another wooden signpost on our right (Wp.5 29M) and cross the first stile but not the second one which would take us into a field. Instead, we go straight ahead (W) up an overgrown sunken track climbing steadily. Fortuitously, the way is heading diagonally up the ridge rather than approaching it head on as we had feared. Where the sunken lane, now doubling as a stream bed, peters out, we are presented with more choices (Wp.6 38M), to the left and straight on there are stiles but we take the rightmost, waymarked route which takes us on the level by the edge of a field (NW).

At the other side of the field, we climb over a gate that has a plank placed across its top to aid us and splash across a stream to enter open moorland. Now climbing again, this time on a grassy path between bracken, there are glorious views of our route continuing diagonally up the ridge and backwards down the valley towards **Longtown**.

After crossing a similar path that is climbing the ridge the other way (Wp.7 51M), we encounter another yellow waymark and a path joins us that's come breathlessly straight up from the valley.

Our route sweeps ninety degrees anti-clockwise (S) so that the valley is now on our left. Continuing to climb steadily, the way remains grassy but eventually flattens out and becomes boggy before we finally attain the ridge at

The 'tombstone' signpost

the **Pile of Stones** (Wp.8 80M). What looks like a small tombstone but is actually a signpost reads 'Olchon Valley' and 'Capel-y-ffin'. **Walk 5 Capel-y-ffin** joins us here from the **Vale of Ewyas** to experience a little of **Offa's Dyke**.

Travellers from all over the world (but particularly the Dutch!) come to spend a fortnight's holiday trudging the length of **Offa's Dyke**. If they appear weary, it's because we have caught them on their longest day, from **Pandy** to **Hay-on-Wye**, not only a seventeen and a half mile trek but requiring them to attain the highest elevation of the fortnight. In comparison, ours is but a jaunt!

Following **Offa's Dyke** to the right (NW), our initial impression is one of beautiful bleakness. Much of the way is muddy, but backbreaking work has been done to cover these areas with large rock slabs forming a pavement, so superior to the railway sleepers covered in chicken wire we found on the **Wicklow Way**! Our path follows the highest point of the wide ridge, level going with fine views of **Crib y Garth** to the right and the **Vale of Ewyas** to the left. Cairns mark where minor paths join us but a much larger cairn (Wp.9 113M) marks the first of two undistinguished summits. Towards the end of the ridge the views open out and we see the trig point at **Hay Bluff** ahead before dropping sharply down to **Llech y Lladron** (Wp.10 140M).

Ignoring the two paved paths ahead, we turn right (SE) to follow a path just below the ridge, alternately muddy and sandy, across the moor's no man's land that typically occurs between heads of valleys, before **Black Hill** can be seen directly ahead. Turning right at a small cairn (Wp.11 155M) onto a smaller path (SSE), we cross more of the same terrain before looking down into the **Olchon Valley** (Wp.12 164M) and being presented with a tricky, rocky path to descend beside the tumbling water of the fledgling river.

After the first part of the descent, the way is such that, although still steadily downward, we can enjoy the vista without worrying about where we place our feet. Crossing a stream that has cut a minor gorge in the hillside (Wp.13 180M) our descent lessens and we pass through a gate onto a track to join a lane that runs around the bottom of the valley (Wp.14 192M). Returning along this pleasant, quiet lane, we turn left (E) up to the car park (Wp.1 220M), that final gradient reminding us of our thoughts when we had set off.

Enjoying the vista on the descent

This route includes **Hay Bluff** and **Lord Hereford's Knob** (also known as **Twmpa**), the two most northerly peaks of the **Black Mountains**, but begins at an altitude of 475 metres so much of the work normally required to enjoy the panoramic views has been done by the car engine before the start is reached. It is very special in that the views in each direction, when walking along the escarpment between them, vary enormously; to the right the patchwork of fields of the **Wye Valley**, to the left the series of **Black Mountain** ridges while ahead are the peaks of the **Brecon Beacons** themselves.

Access by car:
From **Hay-on-Wye**, we head out-of-town towards **Brecon** on the B4350 and, immediately after passing the Swan at Hay, turn left into **Forest Road** signed **Capel-y-ffin**. Ignoring a turning on the right, we see a 'Single track road with passing places' sign and, after a fork right, **Hay Bluff** looms directly ahead and we park the car at its foot on the right. If coming from **Abergavenny**, we can follow the instructions from Route 5 to **Capel-y-ffin** and continue up the mountain road over **Gospel Pass** to approach the car park from the other direction but leave plenty of time as this single track winding road becomes busy in the summer necessitating plenty of reversing!

Hay Bluff

From the car park (Wp.1 0M), we gaze upwards at our first peak **Hay Bluff** before crossing the road and heading directly towards it (SE) across moorland grass between straggly gorse.

Before we've had time to really get our legs going, we must start climbing steeply up the grassy slope but half way up, we are relieved to find that the path swings to the right (S) to climb more steadily diagonally upwards.

Reaching the ridge (Wp.2 34M), we feel we deserve a breather before turning sharp left (NE) and following a gravel path, mercifully on the level, to the trig point at **Hay Bluff** (Wp.3 38M). Its fame is well deserved, with incredible views in every direction.

Retracing our steps (SW), we pass where we attained the ridge (Wp.2 42M) and carry on along the edge of the escarpment. Now we have left the direct route up **Hay Bluff** from the car park, the gravel path has reverted to grass and the way is boggy in places but, to compensate, there are fantastic views plunging down to our right.

Ahead we can see the bluff below **Lord Hereford's Knob**, our second peak, and we easily dismiss various minor paths as our path is several metres wide. Although **Lord Hereford's Knob** is only a few metres higher than **Hay Bluff**, we have to descend right into **Gospel Pass** in order to get there, going gently down with glorious views of the **Vale of Ewyas** opening up to our left.

The bluff below Lord Hereford's Knob

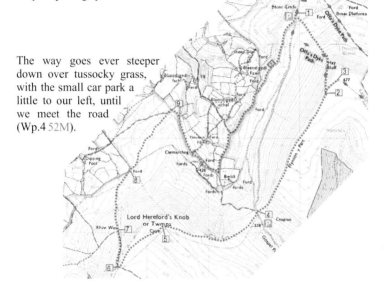

The way goes ever steeper down over tussocky grass, with the small car park a little to our left, until we meet the road (Wp.4 52M).

Across the road and slightly to the left, our way is muddy to start, then steeply climbs with grass underfoot before becoming easier and curving around to the right (W), following the edge of the escarpment again.

The well defined path drifts left up to the diminutive cairn that marks the summit (Wp.5 70M). To our amazement, the views from **Lord Hereford's Knob** are even better than from **Hay Bluff**, no photo can attempt to do them justice; you just have to be here!

The grassy way is seriously steep down the other side (WSW), but becomes easier before meeting a path that crosses ours (Wp.6 86M). We are sad to leave this heavenly path but turn obliquely right and begin to descend the escarpment (N). The path reminds us of our initial climb up **Hay Bluff** as both run diagonally across the incline at a similar gradient. After another path goes off to the left (Wp.7 95M), we descend more steeply and cross a further path, running along the contour, to reach the valley floor.

Presented with a squelchy field and no clear choice of paths, we continue in the same direction heading towards a track that runs on our side of a fence marking the moorland boundary. On reaching the track (Wp.8 110M), we follow it to the right (NE) but after passing the end of a field the way becomes indistinct again. Undaunted, we carry on in the same direction, between windswept hawthorn trees and bracken, making sure that we don't drift too far away from the bottom of the escarpment. Our objective is a lane that runs at right angles to the way we're going, it's not crucial where we hit it.

Reaching this quiet lane (Wp.9 121M), we turn right (SE) and after more open moorland encounter a hawthorn hedge partially hiding land that drops steeply away to our left.

... splashing through fords ...

We're headed to the right of a line below **Gospel Pass**, a direction that seems completely wrong but, just as it seems we must pass through a tunnel beneath it, the lane hairpins to the left (N) and we splash through two fords in quick succession to climb steadily with a mossy, drystone wall on our left before bearing right (NE).

It's an easy yet delightful walk back to the car, as we don't meet any traffic and there are constant views of the escarpment up to our right and the patchwork of fields down to our left. Eventually, we meet the road that's come from **Capel-y-ffin** over **Gospel Pass** and see the car park on our left (Wp.1 161M). There are no refreshments on the route but we return to **Hay-on-Wye** for a late lunch at Oscar's.

5 CAPEL-Y-FFIN

The hamlet of **Capel-y-ffin** has no pub or shop and can only be reached by driving several miles along a single track, winding road from **Hay-on-Wye** at one end or **Llanvihangel Crucorney** at the other. Nevertheless it is the starting point for three of our walks as it is totally surrounded by magnificent ridges and valleys. This is the longest and most strenuous of the three, but shares parts of other walks included here. It starts steeply up onto **Hatterrall Ridge**, sharing part of **Vale of Ewyas** (Walk 6) in reverse, then goes along **Offa's Dyke** to **Hay Bluff**, sharing part of **Hatterrall Ridge** (Walk 3), and **Lord Hereford's Knob**, sharing part **Hay Bluff** (route 4) before making its own way back down the **Nant Bwch** valley to **Capel-y-ffin**.

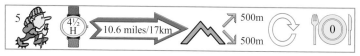

5   H 4½   10.6 miles/17km   500m / 500m   ↻   0

Access by car:
From **Abergavenny** take the A465 towards **Hereford**. After 5 miles, turn left to avoid bypassing the village of **Llanvihangel Crucorney** following signs to **Llanthony Priory**. In the village, turn sharp left after **The Skirrid Inn** and follow signs to **Llanthony**. The ever narrowing road takes us past **Llanthony Priory** and 4 miles later, park on the right hand verge just in front of the village sign for **Capel-y-ffin**.

The white painted church

From the verge (Wp.1 0M) we continue past the village sign (NW), cross a bridge and turn right in front of the white painted church through a blue metal barred gate. A track leads us (NE) across another bridge, with the option of a ford for large vehicles, past a tiny chapel and through a wooden barred gate continually swinging around to the right (SE). We're already steadily climbing up what is now a stony track.

After passing between a barn conversion and an outbuilding we go through another wooden barred gate and already have stunning views right down the valley. We cross a stream, the first of many, which cascades into the river steeply down to our right, then the track disappears and we follow waymark arrows, now on the level, along the bottom of a field. After a stream, we head across the middle of the next field to an elegantly constructed slab stile and continue along the top of the next field to find another creative stile in its top corner (Wp.2 14M).

... an elegantly constructed stile ...

Continuing along the top field edge with a stone building in its bottom corner, we find a more ordinary stile in the top corner which takes us down steep, stone steps, across a stream and along a track with hedges on both sides. The track becomes tarmacked as it passes between buildings and after a rusty barred gate we go slightly down and through a new metal barred gate (Wp.3 22M).

Here we turn back on ourselves, stepping up to a stile on the left and following a signpost 'To The Hill Offa's Dyke' but after only a few paces follow a waymark right over a stream (E) between hawthorns to progress along the bottom of a field. At the corner we follow the path left to steadily climb (N) up the field and over a stile into woodland then steeply up to another stile (Wp.4 31M) into open moorland where we turn right (E). The going is now flat for a bit which gives us the chance to enjoy the views along and across the valley but when we reach a rusty barred gate in the fence running beside us the path swings left to climb steeply between bracken zigzagging up the hill (N).

At one of the hairpins there is a tombstone signpost (Wp.5 43M) and, overall, the path swings to the right (NE) as the gradient becomes less severe and we take a last look back down the valley.

A last look back down the valley

We fork left (Wp.6 52M N) to attain the wide **Hatterrall Ridge** where we can see nothing in any direction which gives an indication of our whereabouts - what a liberating feeling! After patches of bog we meet the **Offa's Dyke** path (Wp.7 59M) and turn left (NW).

Our initial impression is one of beautiful bleakness. At one point the path crosses a lunar-like landscape, requiring frequent cairns to mark our way as the topsoil and any grass have disappeared aeons ago. But much of the way is muddy and backbreaking work has been done to cover these areas with large rock slabs to form a pavement; a 'Trust Upland Erosion Project' board (Wp.8 89M) describes this work.

The path follows the highest point of the wide ridge and the going is on level, with fine views of **Crib y Garth** to the right and the **Vale of Ewyas** to the left but eventually drops down a beautifully laid tessellated pavement to a tombstone signpost at **Llech y Lladron** (Wp.9 119M).

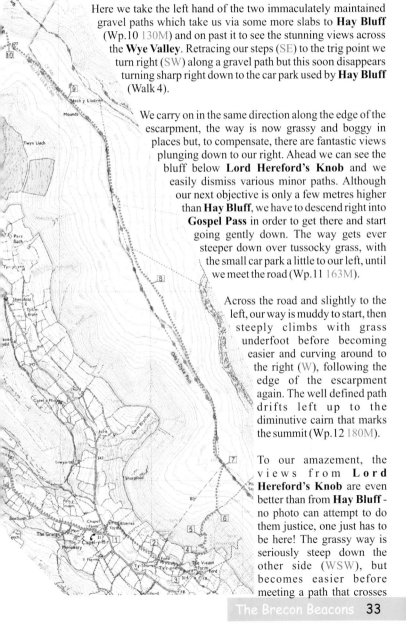

Here we take the left hand of the two immaculately maintained gravel paths which take us via some more slabs to **Hay Bluff** (Wp.10 130M) and on past it to see the stunning views across the **Wye Valley**. Retracing our steps (SE) to the trig point we turn right (SW) along a gravel path but this soon disappears turning sharp right down to the car park used by **Hay Bluff** (Walk 4).

We carry on in the same direction along the edge of the escarpment, the way is now grassy and boggy in places but, to compensate, there are fantastic views plunging down to our right. Ahead we can see the bluff below **Lord Hereford's Knob** and we easily dismiss various minor paths. Although our next objective is only a few metres higher than **Hay Bluff**, we have to descend right into **Gospel Pass** in order to get there and start going gently down. The way gets ever steeper down over tussocky grass, with the small car park a little to our left, until we meet the road (Wp.11 163M).

Across the road and slightly to the left, our way is muddy to start, then steeply climbs with grass underfoot before becoming easier and curving around to the right (W), following the edge of the escarpment again. The well defined path drifts left up to the diminutive cairn that marks the summit (Wp.12 180M).

To our amazement, the views from **Lord Hereford's Knob** are even better than from **Hay Bluff** - no photo can attempt to do them justice, one just has to be here! The grassy way is seriously steep down the other side (WSW), but becomes easier before meeting a path that crosses

The infant Nanat Bwch

ours (Wp.13 195M). Here we turn left onto a much smaller path (SE) but it's still reasonably well defined. It's the typical open moorland that's found at the head of the valley, slight boggy patches interspersed with heather and bilberries. The infant **Nant Bwch** is right by us as we take our first look down the valley that we will follow right back to **Capel-y-ffin**. As we start going gently down the burgeoning stream has grown quickly, fed by a myriad tiny tributaries, and is in a ravine all its own.

The waterfall after Wp.14

Passing between bracken, gorse and hawthorn along the side of the ravine, stepping stones take us across a larger tributary stream (Wp.14 219M) and we spot a picturesque waterfall to our right; the flat, grassy patch beside it would make a great camping site.

At a metal barred gate (Wp.15 231M) we are herded between fences along a track though the gorge containing **Nant Bwch** is still close by. Reaching **Bwaen Bwch Farm** (Wp.16 237M), and going through the pair of gates that contain it, the track becomes tarmacked but passes back into open moorland and the multitude of sheep remind us that there are more of them than us in **Wales**.

It's been gently down all the way so far but after another gate takes us out of moorland (Wp.17 248M) we begin going steadily down between hedges until we cross the river on a high footbridge which indicates how high the water gets. After climbing briefly so that the river is now far down on our left we go steadily down again, passing the **Grange Trekking Centre** on our right before returning to the road at **Capel-y-ffin**. Our car is just to the right (Wp.1 270M).

6 VALE OF EWYAS

We make no apologies for stopping at **Llanthony Priory** for lunch on four walks in this book. Besides being a jewel in itself, it is an oasis in a desert landscape of green when it comes to finding refreshment. And there's nothing to beat a tramp over the hills encountering only the sturdy few, interspersed by the conviviality of a pub lunch. This route starts from the tiny hamlet of **Capel-y-ffin** and goes through farmland and woods in the **Vale of Ewyas** with magnificent views up to the ridges on either side to **Llanthony Priory** then it's up, up, up onto **Hatterrall Ridge** and views over to the next ridge of **Crib y Garth** before the enevitable down, down, down back.

Walks 6 and 7 share their starting points of **Capel-y-ffin** and lunch stops of **Llanthony Priory** so a longer, more strenuous version can be constructed by combining the morning of Walk 7 and the afternoon of Walk 6.

3 | 4H 14M | 8.8 miles/14.1km | 450m / 450m | 4

Access by car:
From **Abergavenny** we take the A465 towards **Hereford** and after 5 miles turn left to avoid bypassing the village of **Llanvihangel Crucorney** following signs for **Llanthony Priory**. In the centre of the village we turn sharp left after **The Skirrid Inn** following signs to **Llanthony**. The ever narrowing road takes us past **Llanthony Priory** and 4 miles later we park on the right hand verge just in front of the village sign for **Capel-y-ffin**.

From the roadside verge (Wp.1 0M) we walk back down the narrow road (SE) between high hedges filled with cow parsley. To the left we can see down to the **Afon Honddu** then up to **Hatterrall Ridge**, our way back this afternoon. To the right we can see glimpses of the equally impressive ridge on the other side of the valley. Variations of these images will accompany us all morning as we proceed pretty much in a continuous direction along the valley. At a white barred gate (Wp.2 6M), we fork right off the road to take a gravel track towards a farmhouse at **Maes-y-ffin**. Here (Wp.3 10M) we go to the left through a new metal barred gate, over a stream and pass to the left of a ruined building into a field. A couple of caravans that look permanently occupied are to our left as we make for the far left hand corner to find a waymarked stile (Wp.4 14M) with rocks neatly positioned as steps.

Continuing along the top of the field edge we go over a stile in it to the left of a new metal barred gate and keep in the same direction passing the remains of a stone building and another permanent looking caravan, this time drab green, on our right. After another metal barred gate we keep to the bottom field edge beside an attractive beech hedge, through a muddy patch and a rusty barred gate to join a track leading to **Penyworld Farm**. In the farmyard (Wp.5 26M) we go left through a gate and immediately right along the top field edge. After a stile you'll be grateful to be this side of the fence as the other side, probably the path's original route, is deep with slurry. Later a stile in the fence takes us back to it, but only when going has improved. Presented with the choice of a new metal gate, a rusty gate or a stile, our way is the stile, across a field then through another metal barred gate to pick our way between nettles,

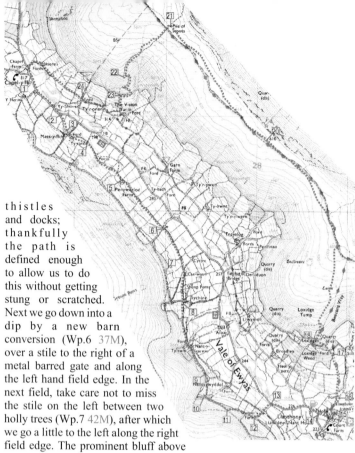

thistles and docks; thankfully the path is defined enough to allow us to do this without getting stung or scratched. Next we go down into a dip by a new barn conversion (Wp.6 37M), over a stile to the right of a metal barred gate and along the left hand field edge. In the next field, take care not to miss the stile on the left between two holly trees (Wp.7 42M), after which we go a little to the left along the right field edge. The prominent bluff above **Llwyn-on** is now opposite us. After a stile to the left of a metal barred gate we enjoy views ahead right down the valley. Keeping a prominent 'No Footpath' sign on a gate to our left, further along the field we pass a water and feeding troughs before arriving at a stile.

The chalet style dwelling

On the other side we pass a farm on our left before a stile to the left of a small wooden gate (Wp.8 50M) with a helpful signpost which confirms not only that we've come from **Capel-y-ffin** but that we're going to **Llanthony**. The well defined path between bracken leads us down (S) to a wooden barred gate, stepping stones across a stream large enough to demand its own name, **Nant y Carnau**, and a handsome chalet style dwelling.

On the other side we pass between another house that's almost hidden and a wooden signpost, to go gently up a delightful, old wooded path with bracken rushing up to our right. To our left we can see beyond the bluff; **Llanthony Priory** is in sight.

Next we come to a stile to the left of a wooden barred gate (Wp.9 66M) that has 'Llanthony' branded into the bar of the stile and continue gently down, past a waymark on a post and can hear a noisy stream ahead. Carrying on along the contour, beside a row of hazel trees, we find a stile to the left of a metal barred gate in the corner of the field (Wp.10 74M). It's now down and across stepping stones then left (ESE) and up the other side through woodland ignoring a path to the left to continue gently up between bracken. Meeting a larger path as it hairpins left on its way up to the ridge (Wp.11 82M E), we turn left and go steadily down it through a metal barred gate to reach a small wooden gate (Wp.12 87M) where we turn left again (NE) to follow a wooden signpost to' Llanthony'.

Continuing steadily down with a dry stone wall to our left we find ourselves between high banks with the way becoming stony as another path crosses us. After a wooden gate the path becomes more like a stream bed which we stumble down in the gloom imposed by overhanging branches. But before long we arrive at the road (Wp.13 94M) where we go right (E). Walking gently downhill we cross **Afon Honddu** back again, pass **The Half Moon** pub, our alternative watering hole, and after a ruined barn on our left turn left off the road though a pair of wooden gates (Wp.14 100M) signed 'Llanthony Priory'. Through another pair of wooden gates we pass the trekking centre on our left and follow around to the left to the priory ruins and the cellar bar (Wp.15 104M), definitely the first choice for lunch. A more substantial lunch can be obtained at **The Abbey Hotel**.

After exploring the stunning ruins, it's time for a bit of effort! We go back past the trekking centre and through the first pair of wooden gates before going right (N) following a signpost 'Circular Walk Hatterrall Hill'. After a wooden gate we go over stepping stones to follow a track signed **Offa's Dyke North** (Wp.16 115M) and then left in front of a mighty yew tree following the general purpose sign of 'Way to Hill'. Over a stile to the left of a gate, we cross a bridge and head straight up the field towards the indent in the ridge ahead. Then in the next field it's slightly to the left towards a mature tree in its corner. To the left of this tree we find a stile (Wp.17 123M) which we cross to enter woodland (NW); but not for long, as after only a few steps it's over another stile into a meadow which we steadily climb to a waymark post where another track crosses us and onto a stile to the left of a small, wooden, padlocked gate with a 'Hatterrall Hill' information board.

... fabulous views to the priory ...

Now we're into open moorland and climbing more steeply between bracken until we reach a flat, grassy terrace (Wp.18 133M); a mega place for a picnic with fabulous views down to the priory. As we go on (N) we need to stop frequently not just because we're out of breath but also to savour the fabulous views. First we look down into the valley then rotate to see our path climbing ever steeper and stonier towards the ridge.

Climbing up to a bluff, you might think you've arrived but it's a false peak and after going down a bit we have to climb steadily up again, but thankfully now it's a less steep grassy path. As the way flattens there are masses of bilberries and after a last look back at **Llanthony Priory**, the way sweeps left, we pass a cairn and can see over to **Hay Bluff**. Eventually, we reach **Offa's Dyke** path (Wp.19 158M) and turn left (NW) by the tombstone signpost.

The path is wide and well defined, a testament to the number of intrepid souls who walk a good part of this long distance footpath which notionally divides England and Wales. **Hatterrall Ridge** is so wide that we are unable to see down into the valleys on either side with only the tops of the ridges visible, but passing another tombstone signpost to 'Red Daren' by a pond, we see the path stretching way ahead of us amidst a sea of heather and birdsong. Where the going is particularly boggy, boulders have been airlifted in for us and in between watching our feet as we step from one to another we raise our eyes and see a trig point ahead (Wp.20 176M) although, strangely, this is not at the highest point. Carrying on, a large cairn marks our arrival at **Pile of Stones** (Wp.21 198M) with the now familiar tombstone sign pointing left to **Capel-y -ffin** and right to **Olchon Valley**. Walk 3 also passes here and we are reminded of the very different weather (as the photos prove) we encountered while researching that route.

Descending into the Vale of Ewyas

Now it's left (SW) along a grassy path that's flat to start with looking down into the **Vale of Ewyas**, but then descends steadily until we reach another tombstone signpost (Wp.22 215M) where we hairpin left (NW) towards a deep gully. We now zigzag steeply down (S), until we reach a rusty barred gate in a fence where we turn right (W) to follow the fence and a row of hawthorns. At a stile in the fence (Wp.23 226M) we go right (S) and down a steep grassy slope through woodland, leaving it in the left bottom corner via a stile. It's steeply down the next field towards a farm on our left and right (W) at the bottom, across a little stream then left (S) following a 'Path legally diverted' sign.

Another stile takes us down some steps to a lane where we go right (WNW) and immediately through a metal barred gate. After going slightly upwards, which doesn't seem right after coming down so far, it becomes a muddy track with hedges on either side but at least now we're going down again. After a stream we climb an amazingly constructed stone stile (Wp.24 245M) and continue along a path by the top of a field. Then it's another creative stile, a field of buttercups, a stile and another stream before we pass between gate posts onto a muddy track. The **Afon Honddu** is far below us on our left as we cross more stepping stones, go through an open wooden barred gate and between a house and its substantial barn to reach a stony track. This sweeps us around to the left (SW), past a tiny wooden chapel and, after a bridge, a white painted church. Through a blue gate we reach the road and turn left (S) to return to our car (Wp.1 254M).

7 BAL MAWR

This route is the pair of Walk 6. Both start at **Capel-y-ffin**, both stop for lunch at **Llanthony Priory** and both have a section of valley walking and a section which climbs up and down a ridge. Both also are a similar distance and involve similar ascents and descents. One difference is that the climb up and down the ridge here is in the morning while that of Walk 6 is after lunch. Perhaps this is why number six, although shorter, has a longer timing! More likely is that the climb up from **Capel-y-ffin** onto the narrow ridge that runs along to **Bal Mawr** is not so steep as the climb up from **Llanthony** onto **Hatterral Ridge**. They can be combined to make a longer, more strenuous version that includes both ridges by combining the morning of Walk 7 with the afternoon of Walk 6.

Access by car:

From **Abergavenny** take the A465 towards **Hereford**. After 5 miles, turn left to avoid bypassing the village of **Llanvihangel Crucorney** following signs to 'Llanthony Priory'. In the village turn sharp left after **The Skirrid Inn** and follow signs to 'Llanthony'. The ever narrowing road takes us past **Llanthony Priory** and 4 miles later, park on the right hand verge just in front of the village sign for **Capel-y-ffin**.

From the verge (Wp.1 0M) we go forward and left up a no-through road signed 'Grange Trekking Centre' (W). Immediately the ridge we will climb is obvious up on our left as we follow the winding lane with a river down on our right. After passing an unusual stile housed in a stone surround we leave the company of the river with **Darren Lwyd** prominent on our right. Turning left (SSW) up a track signed **Grange Trekking** (Wp.2 6M) we climb steadily between a motley collection of old caravans and a house with gothic windows. The way turns sharp left and changes from a track to a muddy footpath with giant steps before we go through a wooden gate and out onto open moorland.

Pony trekkers on our route

Now we zigzag up steeply over stones with a valley opening up to our right and a conifer plantation to our left. As we hairpin left we can see beyond the conifer plantation and right down the **Vale of Ewyas** before crossing a stream on stepping stones, where there's every chance of encountering pony trekkers who've stopped to let their mounts have a drink. Ahead, we can see our way zigzagging up the escarpment.

It's a steep, rocky climb but with fantastic views back. We hairpin right then left (Wp.3 27M), not looking down as the drop is severe, but unconcerned as the path is a metre wide. As it flattens off (S), and is only steadily up, we see our first summit away to our left. Another path joins us on our right that's come along the ridge from **Rhos Dirion** just before we reach a substantial cairn (Wp.4 44M) where we look over into the next valley to see the dam of **Grwyne Fawr Reservoir**. From here the going is flat (SE) then gently climbs to the end of the ridge, which is so narrow that we can see right down into the valleys on either side. Reaching the cairn (Wp.5 58M) that marks our first summit, we stop to look back at the reservoir, across to the substantial conifer plantations and on to **Crug Mawr** and a plethora of lower peaks. Striding along the ridge, you'll feel elated at being on top of the world, though after what seems like no time the trig point at **Bal Mawr** appears (Wp.6 87M).

Trig point at Bal Mawr

Carrying on, the way is extremely well defined; we can see it snaking down to our left as we start steadily down. There's a choice of routes just before a steep bit, but either will do as they come together later.

Alongside Cwm Bwlch

At a cairn (Wp.7 98M) we turn left (NE) and find the path raised above the land either side, no doubt to help drainage. **Cwm Bwlch** opens up to our right and given a choice of routes (Wp.8 104M) we fork right to go steeply down into it between bracken and find ourselves walking along the side of the coomb with a steep drop to our right. This time the path isn't so wide! At a crossroads of paths (Wp.9 120M) we come to a confusing signpost, it correctly points back to **Bal Bach** but indicates **Llanthony** both left and right with **Cwm Bwlch** straight on. The direct way to **Llanthony** is straight on and this is the path we take, over a stile with the ruins now in view.

Through a wooden gate, we go down a field to the left of a farm, cross a track (Wp.10 126M) then over a stile guided by a signpost. Two more stiles separated by a field follow in quick succession. After a gap to the left of the next stile we follow waymarks to the right which take us in just a few steps to another stile and a narrow wooden bridge (Wp.11 131M). Next it's through some woods, across some neatly place stones in mud, over another bridge and down a field following an excess of waymark posts indicating our proximity to civilization. Another stile takes us along the field edge beside **Afon Honddu** then sharp left (NW) to cross it on a metal girder bridge.

Meeting the road (Wp.12 137M), we dink left and right (NE) to reach the priory where we swing around to the right, following signs to car park and toilets, then left into the ruins proper and the cellar bar for our lunch stop (Wp.13 140M). **The Abbey Hotel** is available for a more substantial repast.

Reinvigorated, we retrace our tracks, perhaps looking in the **Church of St. David**, but instead of following the lane around to the left we go straight on (W) through a pair of wooden gates signed 'Capel-y-ffin Road'. Heading to the left of a barn we go through a wooden gate and down some steps to reach the road (Wp.14 143M).

Turning right along it (NW) we pass **The Half Moon** pub and go over two bridges before reaching a signpost on the left (Wp.15 150M) with two pointers reading 'Cwm Bwchel' and 'Way to Hill'. Our way is the latter (SW), even though the path, whilst running between a tunnel of overhanging trees, doubles as a stream bed and we stumble up it to emerge before long at a wooden gate. Continuing steeply upward, the path crosses a track and climbs up between dry stone walls.

Reaching another wooden gate, we turn right (Wp.16 157M WNW), now on the flat, with the hillside stretching up to our left while over a fence to our right a grassy field runs down to the valley floor. After a rusty barred gate we walk between bracken before starting to climb again but where the path hairpins left (Wp.17 162M) we go right and gently down a much smaller path. As the way gets steadily steeper we begin to hear the sound of water before another path joins us on the right and we cross a stream using stepping stones (Wp.18 169M).

The bank on the other side is steep, muddy and a spiny hawthorn is right in our way but, as ever, we cope and it's over a stile to the right of a wooden barred gate (N) to follow the contour by a row of hazel trees. After a waymark on a post we go slightly up between bracken (NNW) and over a stile to the right of a wooden barred gate. Then it's down again (NW) to cross a track and a stream (Wp.19 178M) by a chalet style house to continue through woodland with a fence on our right (N). A pony trekkers' route joins us, the wooden barred gate we go through confirming this with a bridleway sign. After a stile to the left of another wooden barred gate, we pass a farm on our right and enjoy magnificent views ahead. But after the next stile the path disappears!

Our way is past a feeding trough, then a water trough and in the same direction until we see a waymark on a stile to the right of a metal barred gate. This takes us along the top of the next field to find a stile between two hollies (Wp.20 194M). then along the bottom edge of the successive field (NW) with more views opening up ahead. Another metal barred gate leads us to the left of a new barn conversion where we go over a stile but ignore its pair, instead going up a track slightly to the left. Now it's along the bottom of the field edge between stinging nettles, thistles and docks towards a metal barred gate in the corner and along the next two fields in the same manner. Just before reaching a rusty barred gate, we go right over a stile (Wp.21 209M) then left to continue in the same direction and over a stile following the top field edge.

By a farm we follow waymark arrows left through a metal barred gate into its farmyard (Wp.22 213M) then right though another gate out of it. Next we circle left around black plastic-encased hay bales, ignoring the waymark that beckons us down the farm track, to find a rusty gate in the corner of the field (Wp.23 217M). Along the bottom of the next field we pick up a nondescript track which takes us into a low lying, muddy patch and through a metal barred gate to go past a drab green caravan and a ruined stone building.

Over a stile to the right of a metal barred gate (Wp.24 222M) we take the top edge along the next two fields before going through a gap in the far corner of the second field and two gates to the right of a derelict bar, onto a muddy track which, by means of a ford and a gate, takes us to the lane that links **Maes-y-ffin** farm with the valley road. Joining the road via a white barred gate (Wp.25 233M) we turn left to return to our car on the verge in **Capel-y-ffin** (Wp.1 240M).

8 CWMYOY

This route has all the ingredients for a great day out. A reasonably stiff climb affords fantastic views to either side of a ridge before we drop down to a historic monument where there's a choice of refreshment stops. In contrast, the way back is gentle, culminating with the exploration of a fascinating church. And, this is probably the best of the routes in this book that gives easy access to **Llanthony Priory** as a lunchtime stop. After climbing **Hatterrall Hill** to reach **Offa's Dyke Path**, we descend to the priory before returning through woods on the other side of the **Vale of Ewyas** to the famous, crooked **Cwmyoy Church**.

Access by car:
From **Abergavenny** take the A465 towards **Hereford**. After 5 miles, turn left to avoid bypassing the village of **Llanvihangel Crucorney**, following signs to 'Llanthony Priory'. In the village, turn sharp left after **The Skirrid Inn** and turn right immediately after **The Red Lion** public house, down a tiny lane signposted 'Cwmyoy'. At a T-junction turn left then fork left to spot **Cwmyoy Church** ahead. In the hamlet itself turn right, then swing left up beside a white cottage to park above the church.

From our position above the church (Wp.1 0M) we head up a footpath (N) immediately opposite following a signpost reading 'Graig 0.1km'. The steep, rocky path is completely overgrown overhead, resembling a dark tunnel; you might wonder whether a riddle needs solving before we may pass an ancient, gnarled oak tree. The way broadens to a sunken lane and the spell is broken after we pass through a green painted gate to reach a bright, modern 'Welcome to Hatterrall Hill' Information Board (Wp.2 9M) and turn right (E). After our early exertion the way ahead with a dry stone wall on our right is easy, skirting impressive rock crags to our left (N), unnamed on the map. A path to the left (Wp.3 16M) tempts us but our way is straight on the flat, then over a stile left of a rickety wooden gate (NE) before, surprisingly, going gently downhill with lovely views across the valley to **Ysgyryd Fawr**. To the left it's steeply up, but our objective, **Hatterrall Ridge**, is straight ahead. Immediately after a large yellow painted house (Wp.4 22M) the main path swings right towards the valley bottom while we carry along the contour towards it.

A stile, right of a wooden barred gate, takes us just above the valley floor with sublime views across it. After another stile, we ignore a further path on the left (Wp.5 35M) which might tempt us onto the ridge, but for now can revel in descending gently - our climb will come soon enough. After a gate we cross a stream, turn sharp right then, before reaching a stile, turn sharp left to start climbing steeply up a wide grassy path (NNE). Just before reaching a dry stone wall topped with a fence the path turns right (SE). The climbing is now just steady as we swing around to the left (E). After a metal barred gate (Wp.6 47M), the path swings further left (NE) and it's steeply up again to a fork (Wp.7 58M) to take the right, steeper option (ENE) towards the top of the ridge, curving slowly left (NNW) between bilberries and heather, then dropping down the other side of the wide ridge with wide views to the east,

Offa's Dyke Path stretches ahead

before reaching **Offa's Dyke Path** (Wp.8 76M), stretching away into the distance as we turn left. We follow it right (NNE) and the distinctive ruins of **Llanthony Priory** soon come into view. The next path left is surprisingly, not the way down to them; it's at the tombstone signpost indicating 'Llanthony' left and 'Longtown' right where we leave the long distance footpath (Wp.9 97M NW).

This path takes us gently down the valley side alongside a drystone wall. The priory disappears behind a bluff as the way becomes steeper and rockier, gorse impeding our progress, to reappear before we turn left through a metal barred gate (Wp.10 125M), where we negotiate a damp patch before heading half right across a field, gently down towards a wood with great views of **Llanthony Priory**. Undeterred by a stream and thistles, we enter a wood via a metal barred gate (Wp.11 131M) where our path becomes a track which bends left (W) as it's joined by another. A second gate takes us out of the wood; the obvious path goes straight ahead but we follow a waymark across to the field's right hand corner and find a wooden gate (Wp.12 140M) taking us right onto a track. Although adjacent to the ruins, we must make our way past them and keep turning left to attain our lunchtime stop at the cellar bar (Wp.13 156M).

Having satisfied the inner man (or woman) we go back past **Llanthony Church** and follow the vehicular route (SW) to the road running along the valley; we go straight across then diagonally left (SSE) along a path to a metal bridge across the **Afon Honddu** (Wp.14 161M). Then it's straight on, ignoring the way right signposted 'Bal Bach', across a stile into a field. Our way isn't the obvious path; it's along the right hand field edge (SE) to a yellow waymark where we splash through a stream and up a clearly defined path to the right (S) and a stile (Wp.15 168M). Here it's half right (W) up to another stile in the field's corner to join a stony track. In a few strides we turn left onto an overgrown path (Wp.16 171M SE) and through a wooden gate. After an initially unpromising section between stinging nettles, we go over a stile into a wood and after ignoring a path to the right continue through fragrant bracken. After passing a surprisingly empty dwelling in need of rescuing, we go through a metal barred gate and reaching a track that hairpins in front of us (Wp.17 181M). The right hand option takes us steadily up between widely spaced conifers to pass **Graig-Ddu Cottage** on our right, whereupon our way reverts to a muddy path before reaching a large track (Wp.18 189M).

Turning right (S), we march along enjoying lovely views along the valley. The track bends around to the right (SW) to reach a cattle grid; we then leave the track where it swings further to the right (Wp.19 196M) for a footpath beside a barbed wire fence. This takes us muddily down to a stream where several paths come together; our way is forward (S) through a metal barred gate and alongside a wood. We enjoy views across the valley to the cliffs of **Darren**, leaving the wood behind after two more metal barred gates to cross some stones and join another large track. But not for long; as we pass **Noyaddllwyd Farm** our route is the overgrown footpath on the left (Wp.20 217M) that follows the elegant dry stone wall marking the perimeter of their garden. Crossing a stile, we follow the right hand field edge along the contour as

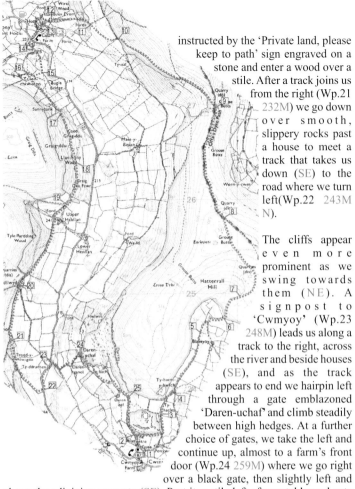

instructed by the 'Private land, please keep to path' sign engraved on a stone and enter a wood over a stile. After a track joins us from the right (Wp.21 232M) we go down over smooth, slippery rocks past a house to meet a track that takes us down (SE) to the road where we turn left(Wp.22 243M N).

The cliffs appear even more prominent as we swing towards them (NE). A signpost to 'Cwmyoy' (Wp.23 248M) leads us along a track to the right, across the river and beside houses (SE), and as the track appears to end we hairpin left through a gate emblazoned 'Daren-uchaf' and climb steadily between high hedges. At a further choice of gates, we take the left and continue up, almost to a farm's front door (Wp.24 259M) where we go right over a black gate, then slightly left and above the adjoining property (SE). Past it, a stile left of a metal barred gate takes us onto a path following a fence on our right with bracken, gorse and brambles on our left.

The path broadens as we head towards farm buildings; before reaching them, a stile to the left takes us steadily up a sunken lane to a wooden barred gate (Wp.25 279M). The path appears to go right in front of it into a field, but our way is through the gate into a wood alongside a dry stone wall (S). After passing an out of place wooden chalet on the left, a track joins us up from the right and we meet our outgoing route (Wp.2 290M). Turning right, we stumble down the rocky path that spooked us earlier, back to the car (Wp.1 295M). The amazing crooked church deserves exploration before the end of our day.

The amazing crooked church

9 PONT CADWGAN

Grwynne Fawr Valley must be the best kept secret of the **Black Mountains**. It is narrower and more wooded than its two sisters, the **Vale of Ewyas** and **Olchon Valley**, to the east and, as the access instructions below demonstrate, is more difficult to find. This route goes over the ridge between it and the **Vale of Ewyas**, wandering through woodland for much of the way, to break at **Llanthony Priory** for lunch then returns more directly, climbing up **Cwm Bwchel** to cross the open moorland landscape of **Bal Bach** in the afternoon.

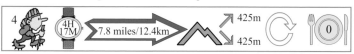

Access by car:

From **Abergavenny** take the A465 towards **Hereford**. After 5 miles, turn left to avoid bypassing the village of **Llanvihangel Crucorney** following signs to 'Llanthony Priory'. In the village, turn sharp left after **The Skirrid Inn** and left again at the first choice following signs to 'Llanthony', but in the village of **Stanton** turn left signed 'Forest Coal Pit, Partrishow' and 'Llanbedr'. At a five way cross roads follow the white lines, which strangely lead towards none of these places but to **Grwynne Fawr Reservoir**. One mile after a sign announcing 'Mynydd Du Forest', after the road widens on the right, turn right to cross a narrow bridge and circle around to the right to find a delightful, though not signed, car park.

From the car park at **Pont Cadwgan** (Wp.1 0M), from which this walk takes its name, we pass between green metal posts and turn right to walk along a track (E) on the flat. Passing a green barrier we climb steadily amidst dense, green conifers until we arrive at **Cadwgan Farm** (Wp.2 7M) where we follow the public footpath sign which leads us slightly to the right down between dry stone walls.

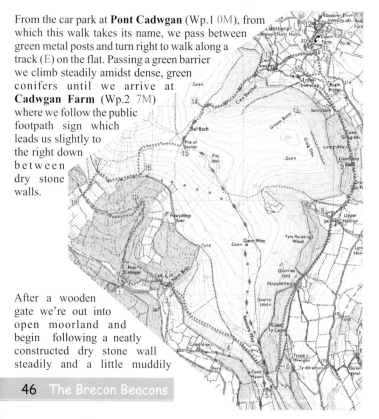

After a wooden gate we're out into open moorland and begin following a neatly constructed dry stone wall steadily and a little muddily

upwards. Where the main path hairpins left away from the wall (Wp.3 13M) we follow it but drift right (SE) between bracken and foxgloves. The view of the other side of the valley with conifers marching up the hill is stunning and you might spot sheep sheltering from the sun under hawthorn trees, seemingly unappreciative of the idyll that is their world.

A larger, grassy track joins us from the left (Wp.4 25M) and we enjoy brilliant views of **Twyn y Gaer** straight ahead as we walk on with a fence, then a dry stone wall to our left. Down to the right we can see the road that brought us to the start and as we leave the shadow of the dry stone wall the rocky escarpment below **Hatterrall Hill** comes into view. After another grass track joins us from the left we come to some stones carefully arranged to form a phallic sculpture (Wp.5 48M).

The phallic sculpture at Wp.5

Magnificent views of the Vale of Ewyas

Here we go left, then within a few paces left again (N) to go steeply down a narrow but well-defined path between bracken with magnificent views ahead of the **Vale of Ewyas**.

Reaching a wide, metalled track (Wp.6 53M) we turn left and proceed through woods on the level. After a cattle grid we pass **Noyaddllwyd Farm** to our right then, before reaching a second cattle grid, take care to leave the track (Wp.7 66M) to take a path on the right (NE). This takes us through bracken, over a stream and across stepping stones to a metal barred gate. Next it's along the edge of a wood with trees stretching over us and through a rusty gate before coming to the wooden barred gate that takes us out from under the trees so that we see a coomb, the English version of *cwm*, to our left. Coming to a ford (Wp.8. 81M) we go left and then right up a stony track. At the top there are a choice of ways but either will do because they both join another wide metalled track and after passing to the side of a cattle grid we enter **Llanthony Wood**.

Where the track starts sweeping to the right and going down (Wp.9 94M) we turn left (N) onto a minor, muddier track but after **Graig-ddu Cottage** it markedly improves. However, soon it hairpins right and we carry straight on (NW) following a wooden signpost along another muddy track, but now with lovely views to our right. After passing a surprisingly unoccupied cottage on our left we cross a stile with 'Llanthony' branded into it (Wp.10 113M) and go sharp right (ENE) onto a track. Within fifty metres a stile on our left takes us (E) down the middle of a field to a stile, then diagonally across the next field

(NNW) to the left corner where we ford a stream and continue along the left field edge to find a metal girder bridge (Wp.11 120M) that crosses the **Afon Honddu**. Meeting the valley road we spot the lane opposite which leads to **Llanthony Priory** (NE) where we swing right and then left into the ruins proper, and our lunchtime rendezvous with the cellar bar (Wp.12 126M).

Having satisfied the inner man (or woman) we retrace our steps back to the metal girder bridge (Wp.11 131M) and this time turn right (W) along the edge of the river. After a stile we go steadily up a field following waymark posts to another stile that takes us across a muddy gully following a signpost to **Cwm Bwchel**. Then it's through woods, across a narrow wooden bridge and left through a gap in the hedge beside a stile and up two more fields to cross a track (Wp.13 145M) to the right of a farm. A wooden gate above the farm is a good place to stop, not only to look back at the magnificent view of the priory but also to prepare for the challenging climb ahead.

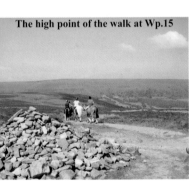

The high point of the walk at Wp.15

After a stile we reach a crossroad of paths and signpost which indicates **Bal Bach**, our next objective, straight on, then it's steeply up the side of **Cwm Bwchel** (WSW) between bracken. Eventually, after swinging right (WNW) and cracking the steepest part of the climb, a path joins us from the right (Wp.14 180M) and we continue (SW), now only climbing steadily, on a raised path across the moorland to reach a cairn (Wp.15 197M), the highest point of our walk.

At this meeting of ways we carry straight on with the path swinging right (W) before going steeply down and we enjoy splendid views of the forested **Grwynne Fawr Valley**, even though it's somewhat marred by the scars left where areas of forest have been cleared. At a fork we take the right option that heads down towards a conifer plantation but overall the path still manages to take us left (S). Reaching the plantation (Wp.16 209M) and unwilling to plumb its seemingly impenetrable depths, we turn right (W) along a substantial track and after passing the corner of the plantation a wide grassy path crosses us (Wp.17 219M). Here we turn left (SW) down to a waymarked stile, followed quickly by another to our left after which we turn right to cross a field to a third stile and find another well-used track (Wp.18 223M). Now it's left (SE) first into an area where trees have been felled and then into what feels like a proper forest. The track turns steadily to the left (NE), watching out for the point where it widens (Wp.19 238M) because here we take a path which drops down from the track to the right, travelling in almost the same direction. It swings tightly right around to the right (S) to take us down a delightful woodland path beside the gurgling **Nant y Gwerydd**. At the bottom we turn left just before the bridge to find our car (Wp.1 257M).

find a footpath on our left (S) with a stile left of a metal barred gate with 'Golden Grove' on it.

The massive oak at Wp.11

After another gate we pass between a house and its outbuildings with indications that the area is used for camping, then through another gate into a field with **Grwynne Fawr**, which we're following, tumbling and gurgling to our left. Our way goes over a stile into a flower bedecked meadow then over another stile into woodland with the sound of the river never far away. A stile by a massive oak (Wp.11 136M) takes us onto a lane where we turn left (SE) over a bridge and, sadly, leave the river. After passing between beautifully manicured gardens that straddle the lane we meet a road (Wp.12 140M) and turn right (S) to continue along the valley.

But not for long, at the first turning on the left (Wp.13 144M) the gentle walking which we've enjoyed since our lunchtime stop has to end.

The lane climbs steadily (E) to start, with the jumble of buildings which make up **Hall Farm** on our right but then becomes steeper between hedges and a wooded valley opens up on our right with a conifer plantation on the other side. The lane deteriorates into a track that swings sharp left (N) and almost immediately we are confronted with two metal barred gates (Wp.14 155M). But we turn sharp right (E) through neither of them, following a public footpath sign towards a new barn conversion in a fantastic position. The track goes immediately to its left and continues gently upwards with **Sugar Loaf** appearing ahead, a fence on our left and a field dropping away into the valley on our right. Topping the rise after the long continual climb up from **Llangenny**, we start dropping before meeting a footpath quaintly signed 'Way to Hill' which goes up to the left (Wp.15 165M). However, we to continue gently down to the valley bottom. But after passing through a metal barred gate and, crossing a stream, the track swings right (SSE) and it's up again to pass a refreshingly un-modernised cottage with a half slate, half corrugated iron roof.

Swinging right (SW), a green canopy is provided by mature oaks on either side before we approach a diagonal crossroad of tracks (Wp.16 174M), still heading straight on and on steadily up now between statuesque beeches. Where the track swings left (SE) it becomes metalled and flattens pleasingly to pass though farmland again. At a further junction of tracks (Wp.17 184M) we turn left to pass the higgledy-piggledy collection of farm buildings and general detritus that makes up **Pen-y-graig**, to see our car way ahead and across to the right. Passing through several open gates, it's clear that this track is used to provide east-west access between local farms. The next of these is **Llyweddrog** (Wp.18 194M) with a closed metal barred gate. We pass into open moorland and enjoy views across the **Usk Valley** to **Blorenge** before reaching the car park (Wp.1 199M). The terrace of **The Sugar Loaf Vineyard** is recommended for a relaxed refreshment stop.

When you first climb **Sugar Loaf** from the more usual **Usk Valley** side (Route 14) and look down from the summit, you'll spot the path that this route follows, climbing up from the valley. Bet you couldn't wait! Our route starts north east of **Sugar Loaf** and zigzags to the summit, before going west to reach **Grwyne Fawr**, then returning along its valley to the north of the mountain.

3 | 4H | 9.5 miles/15km | ↗375m ↘375m | 0*

*but there's a pub in **Pantygelli** 2.4km (1½ miles) from the start

Access by car:
Coming from **Abergavenny**, take the road that runs north from the A40 signed to 'The Hill College' and 'Leisure Centre' named **Penypound**. After two and a half miles you reach **Pantygelli** and fork left, and after another mile, pass through the village of **Bettws**. Half a mile further on, after passing **Upper Bettws Farm** on the right you'll reach a gravel car park on the left. Perversely, despite the entrance not being obvious, there's no signpost to it. However, you'll know you're in the right place, as there is an obvious footpath from it signed 'Sugar Loaf'.

Starting from the car park (Wp.1 0M), we follow the direction of the signpost up a grassy path between hedges (W) and pass through a kissing gate to the right of a wooden five-barred gate (Wp.2 3M). Ten metres further on we turn left back on ourselves (SE) between bracken, and soon meet a wire fence atop a drystone wall on our left, over which there are glorious views of the valley.

Climbing steadily upwards with gorse and heather sprouting from the wall, we reach a metal five-barred gate (Wp.3 10M) and fork right opposite it (SW), up a grassy path between bracken. As the path flattens out we get our first glimpse of the summit, its distinct outline immediately ahead.

Another drystone wall appears in front us (Wp.4 14M); though it seems we should go over it, our route takes us (NW) parallel and ten metres to its right. Now the views of the valley are on our right, as we've swung through 180 degrees. Meeting a path that comes up more steeply from the valley (Wp.5 24M), we turn left (SW) and climb again, keeping a drystone wall to our left.

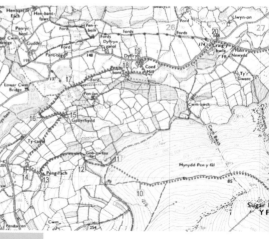

At the corner of the enclosed field, we follow the wall around to the left (S), the panoramic views of the valley switching to the left again. We take a fork to the right (Wp.6 28M SW) on a smaller grassy path which goes gently upwards between bracken, passing the gnarled remains of a hawthorn hedge before becoming steeper and topping a ridge. Ahead is a strangely solitary gate with no fencing attached either side, its sign (Wp.7 40M) indicating that the National Trust have created a diversion to protect the original 7th century path from becoming severely eroded - this has been created by cutting a three metre swathe through the heather, not making the easiest walking conditions. Passing a pond on our right crammed full with bulrushes, we can see **Hay Bluff** in the distance. Another solitary gate indicates the end of the diversion (Wp.8 51M), and now the route gets increasingly steep.

Magnificent views from the trig point

After crossing a path that follows the contour around **Sugar Loaf**, we clamber over rocks to reach the summit (Wp.9 64M). The rocky plateau is topped with the customary trig point by which walkers have the obligatory photos taken. It's no surprise that the climb us here is popular, as the views are magnificent in every direction.

Crossing to the far side of the plateau, we negotiate large boulders before walking down a wide grass path (NW) that's so smooth, it looks as though it has been mown. Passing a couple of dew ponds on the right, our way bears gently left (W) and we continue in this direction along a wide ridge ignoring several alternatives to our left. Here, as elsewhere in the **Brecon Beacons**, there is a distinct line where the gorse, bilberries and heather change to bracken; we keep to the right again (Wp.10 99M) before descending quite steeply to reach a distinct green crossroads (Wp.11 107M).

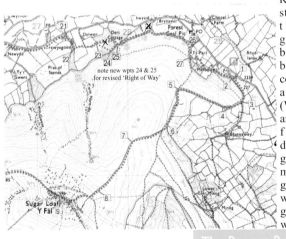

Keeping straight down this wide, grassy path between bracken, we come to a gap in a rustic fence (Wp.12 111M) and turn right in front of a drystone wall to go through a metal barred gate (N). The way is now a grassy track which twists right and left, becoming stony. Passing through a new metal barred gate into a wood, we follow a leaf-strewn track which leaves the wood to pass between high hedges. The track comes out into a lane (Wp13 120M); to the left are farm buildings, but we go right (NW), almost immediately passing a well made private road that forks to the left. At the next farm (Wp14 122M), we climb a stile to our right and cross the field at right angles to the lane (N) to make for a yellow waymark in the hedge opposite where we find another stile with a big drop into the next field. Crossing to the far corner, we climb a reinforced fence into woodland; the route is not obvious here, but by keeping parallel to the fence on our right, we soon see another yellow waymarked stile. Avoiding a ditch on the other side we make for the next stile and waymark from where we have a good view of **Llanbedr** nestling in the valley to our left - a good place for a picnic.

Then it's over yet another stile and along the left side of the next field into an orchard with the subtle sign 'Please don't pick these apples, they do not belong to you'. Arriving at a lane with grass in the middle (Wp.15 133M) we turn sharp left (W) and immediately after leaving the grounds of **Gettyrhydd Farm** take a rocky track to our right (Wp.16 135M NW) signed 'Pen y Bont', which drops down, bends to the right (NE) and becomes a path between high hedges for a while. Then it's a sunken lane through woods which feels like it hasn't changed since the Middle Ages. We hear and then see **Grwyne Fawr** down to our left. Ahead, the way divides (Wp.17 144M), the main route going down to the left to cross the river at a ford, but we carry straight on over a little stream and on to a wooden gate that can be opened from horseback. Our route continues along this ancient way until we rejoin civilization with a new wooden gate (Wp.18 155M), a man-made pond to our left and a restored house to our right. Joining the tarmac strip that leads from house to road, we cross the river and follow its left hand bank before turning away from it up to the road that runs along the valley (Wp.19 162M).

The picturesque stone bridge

Here we turn right (E) and stride along, forking right (Wp.20 173M) to follow the signpost to 'Fforest' and 'Abergavenny' and cross the river again at a picturesque stone bridge. After passing the substantial **Trewyscoed House** we look for a signpost and stile in the hedge to our right (Wp.21 185M S).

Short Cut
Alternatively, if your legs are tiring, continue along the road keeping right at any junctions until arriving back at our starting point .

Climbing up the left hand side of the field, we cross a stile half way up and the way becomes steeper before we reach another stile at the top (Wp.22 191M). Here we turn left onto a track (E) which soon degenerates into a path across a field. The way here is not obvious but making toward the far right hand corner of the field we find the path again where a little stream runs beneath local overhead power cables and cross it on randomly placed stones to reach a stile (Wp.23 195M). Following the path up the right side of the scrubby field, we cross another stile then go diagonally right (SE) up to a third stile (Wp.24 197M).

Here it's left (E) along a more established path to a wooden gate - the rear entrance to Deri Cottage (Wp.25 199M). We go up to the right through woodland, following a prominent new sign, first with a dry stone wall to our left while working our way around the property and then with a fence separating us from a succession of fields (E). Continuing in the same direction, the path dives down away from the field boundary through the woodland then steeply up before rejoining the boundary between wood and field and we continue on to a National Trust sign announcing **Sugar Loaf** and **Pen-y-Fal** (Wp.26 215M).

Here we turn right (S) and climb steeply up the hill beside a fence on our left, looking for an easily missed stile in it (Wp.27 220M) which takes us (SE) initially to the right of a dry stone wall and then to the left of the remains of an old stone building. Navigating a stile to the right of a black painted gate, a track and a wooden gate in quick succession, we continue along the bottom of a field noticing a house with ducks and chickens in the garden to our left. A curious double gate tries to bar our way but we foil its intricacies and pass along the bottom of the next field with the ubiquitous dry stone wall to our left until finding ourselves back at the wooden gate (Wp.2 235M) and thence to the car park (Wp.1 238M).

This ascent of **Sugar Loaf**, eye-catching itself from every direction, has great views not only from the top but also on both ascent and descent. Instead of the traditional lower route up from the **Llwyn Du** car park past **Porth-y-parc** farmhouse, it immediately makes for the higher ground, climbing straight up onto **Rholben** ridge and after attaining the summit comes back along **Deri** ridge, returning through ancient oak woodland.

3	2H 41M	5.2 miles/8.3km	350m 350m		0*

* 4 for the longer alternative

Access by car:

Coming from **Abergavenny**, we take **Chapel Road**, which runs north from the A40 just the town side of the roundabout with the A4143. It appears to be purely residential, with a 20 mph speed limit and speed bumps, but we start to climb as we leave the town, passing a staggered crossroad and a 'No Through Road' sign. After just two miles where it degenerates into a track, we find the **Llwyn Du** car park on our right which has beautiful views across the valley.

Alternative Route

A longer alternative can be made by joining with part of **Bryn Arw** (Route 17). Branch off left at Wp.10 to join Walk 17 at its Wp.24, then follow it past its start/end point to Wp. 21. Then go straight on to rejoin Walk 16 at its Wp.13.

At the car park (Wp.1 0M), we find a notice informing us that the summit of **Sugar Loaf** is reached by taking the track uphill to our right through **Porth-y-parc** farmyard.

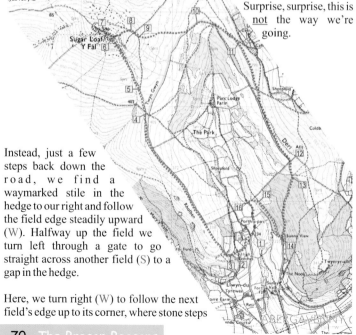

Surprise, surprise, this is <u>not</u> the way we're going.

Instead, just a few steps back down the road, we find a waymarked stile in the hedge to our right and follow the field edge steadily upward (W). Halfway up the field we turn left through a gate to go straight across another field (S) to a gap in the hedge.

Here, we turn right (W) to follow the next field's edge up to its corner, where stone steps lead up to a stile (Wp.2 7M).

Right and immediately left takes us up through a wood behind the farmhouse, to a stile in its right hand corner (Wp.3 11M). The tricky navigation is now over as we are out onto open moorland with fantastic views of **Blorenge** across the valley and **Abergavenny** down to our right. Turning right (NW), we join the main path that climbs steeply up from the valley floor. We are now on **Rholben** ridge which we'll follow to the summit.

Sugar Loaf ahead

Initially, we walk beside a fence but where the path divides we choose the steeper, left-hand alternative veering away from it, a wide, grassy path between bracken with a little gorse and a few isolated hawthorn trees. Where the path flattens, it runs beside a low drystone wall, this time supplemented by a hedge, and we can see **Sugar Loaf** ahead with **Cibi Valley** down to our right and **Deri** ridge beyond it. Soon after ignoring a diagonal path to our right and another joining us from the left, a major path crosses ours (Wp.4 42M) and we begin to climb again, ignoring a less steep track to our right (Wp.5 47M) and crossing a stream in a gully.

... steeper and rockier ...

The way gets steeper and rockier, the fantastic views all around allowing us an excuse for plenty of stops. After joining another route to the top (Wp.6 65M), we ignore a very steep path to our right before emerging, without much warning, at the trig point (Wp.7 70M). At the right hand end of the small plateau, we drop down steeply to the left (E) with panoramic views, best enjoyed when stationary! After the initial steep descent, we turn right where a path crosses us (Wp.8 79M) to follow the contour and then turn left (Wp.9 81M), steeply and then more gently down between heather, savouring views of **Ysgyryd Fawr** directly ahead and **Deri** ridge to our right.

On meeting a boundary of hedge and fence enclosing trees, we turn left to join a path that runs by it and reach a smaller path that forks left (Wp.10 91M).

N.B. The longer alternative route branches off here.

We carry on around the enclosure until we pass an entrance to it with a National Trust sign 'Parc Lodge'. The path now becomes wide and grassy as it makes for the top of **Deri** ridge, and where it divides (Wp.11 101M), we take the right fork (SE) with views into the valleys left and right. At each subsequent division we keep right, moving close to a drystone wall which becomes completely encased in moss and is eventually replaced by a fence. Reaching the corner of the enclosure (Wp.12 120M), we cross another path and go a little to our right (SSE), down between gorse.

At a meeting of ways (Wp.13 123M), we welcome the longer alternative route back, and go slightly to the right again (SSW), gently down along a beautiful path between gnarled oaks with a carpet of leaves underfoot. After passing a spring which produces a stream that crosses our path and then runs beside us, the way becomes sunken until we suddenly emerge from this fairy tale land to find habitation (Wp.14 138M).

The path between gnarled oaks

We can see our starting point across the valley, but our route takes us up and down it before getting there. We turn obliquely right opposite the first house through a rusty gate (NW), to re-enter the wood on a delightful path with a stream tumbling over rocks below us getting ever louder. Passing through a kissing gate with an NT waymark, the way becomes a track reinforced with slate, and we climb steadily again. Before this becomes too irksome, we follow another NT waymark atop a post left (Wp.15 149M) onto a path which descends to a stream. Fording this and climbing up the other side, we reach a track (Wp.16 154M), turn left (SE) and return to the car park (Wp.1 161M).

The stream between Wps. 15 & 16

There are no refreshments on the route but **Abergavenny** is only two miles away or, alternatively, we can recommend a visit to the cafe of **Sugar Loaf Vineyard** (turn right at the staggered crossroads).

It may not be the best known hilltop in the **Black Mountains**, but **Bryn Arw** offers glorious views of **Ysgyryd Fawr** to the east, **Blorenge** to the south, **Sugar Loaf** to the west and the **Vale of Ewyas** with its attendant peaks to the north. This route combines **Bryn Arw** in the morning and **Deri** ridge and the south-eastern flank of **Sugar Loaf** in the afternoon, with **The Crown** in **Pantygelli** being the meat in the sandwich. The chance of a decent pub half way around a worthwhile walk is not common enough in this area - don't miss it!

A shorter alternative
After ascending **Bryn Arw**, return along the road from the pub in **Pantygelli**.

Access by car:
Coming from **Abergavenny**, take the road that runs north from the A40 signed to 'The Hill College' and 'Leisure Centre' named **Penypound**. After two and a half miles we reach **Pantygelli** and fork left. After another mile we pass through the village of **Bettws**, and half a mile further on after passing **Upper Bettws Farm** on our right, reach a gravel car park on our left. Perversely, despite the entrance not being obvious, there is no signpost to it. However, you'll know you're in the right place if there's an obvious footpath from it signed 'Sugar Loaf', even though it's not on our agenda today.

From the car park (Wp.1 0M), we walk back down the lane (SE), hilltops all around us. Reaching a tarmacked track on our left signed 'Bettws Farm' (Wp.2 3M), we make our way towards the farm (N) until the track turns sharp right (Wp.3 7M) where we go straight on (NW) over a stile, with a yellow waymark to the right of a green metal gate. A pond on the corner has flooded over the unmade track, so our way though scrubby woodland is wet until it rises and becomes more pleasant.

After the track swings right, we pass out of the wood through a new metal gate (Wp.4 12M), to progress up the right hand side of a field and round the top of it, then passing through a gap in the hedge by a large holly. To the left, across a field, we can now see what would be an attractive stone barn (if it didn't have a rusty corrugated iron roof) and make straight towards it, crossing a stile in front of it (Wp.5 17M) to follow a track on the barn's right down towards **Old Coalpit Farm**.

At a T-junction (Wp.6 23M) we turn right (NE) onto another track, pass the farm on our left and go over a stile to the left of a metal gate with the rounded hilltop of **Twyn y Gaer** prominent on the other side of the valley. Our way becomes a sunken lane, looking like an ancient greenway, and ignoring a lane to our left, we follow a signpost to 'Stanton'. It's sad to see the drystone wall to our right repaired with old pieces of gate, but perhaps the pressures of farming can make such moves expedient. Climbing steadily, with the lower slopes of **Sugar Loaf** behind us, we pass over a stile by a gate into open moorland (Wp.7 33M).

Forking right (SSW), we begin to climb steeply up a wide grassy path which circles to the right to join and then follow another drystone wall. After the wall changes to a fence we continue climbing steadily but, by three trees in the fence (Wp.8 41M), turn left onto a smaller path which snakes steeply up (E) to attain the ridge (Wp.9 46M) by a lone thorny tree. After looking back down the **Vale of Ewyas,** with **Crug Mawr** and **Hatterrall Hill** guarding each side, we continue along its backbone, passing old quarry workings (SSE) until we reach two cairns on our left (Wp.10 61M) which indicate where we must leave the main path to travel down **Bryn Arw's** eastern flank (SE).

Dropping steeply down towards the village of **Blaengavenny** with **Ysgyryd Fawr** beyond, we eventually meet a fence (Wp. 11 75M).

Here we turn right onto a path overhung with trees, that runs along the contour and reaching a fork where the main path goes up onto the

... towards the village of Blaengavenny with Ysgyryd Fawr beyond ...

ridge (Wp.12 84M), we continue to follow the fence (S) which now reinforces a line of mature trees. The sound of a train reminds us of how surreally close we are to both the railway line and dual carriageway that run between **Abergavenny** and **Hereford**.

At the southern end of **Bryn Arw**, we sweep to the right (W) and go steeply down towards the sound of a river which we must cross.

To our right is a fairy tale glen with an inviting footpath but this is not our way, instead we cross a stile in the fence to our left and go down to roughly positioned stepping stones

(Wp.13 109M) then up from the river, obliquely left (S), beside a plantation of conifers. At the corner of the plantation, we go over a stile beside a gate, with barbed wire cruelly wound across its top, and cross a field to three gates (Wp.14 117M). The rightmost has a stile with a waymark but, not seduced, we take the leftmost gate and follow a track (ESE) down to the road (Wp.15 127M). A brisk walk along to our right (SW), passed the village sign to 'Pantygelli' and a garage on the corner where we join the road we'd driven up earlier brings us to our lunchtime stop (Wp.16 137M).

The Crown is an unexpected find with draught Grolsch and coffee from a real espresso machine, the quality of the food and beer garden showing similar enterprise.

If you stay longer than intended, you can return directly to the car park along the road, remembering to fork left at the garage - but those of us made of sterner stuff we continue along the road (S) until we meet a sunken lane with a 'No Through Road' sign up to our right (Wp.17 140M). Plodding steadily uphill (WSW) with holly to our right, it's a relief to turn left beside a high wall enclosing a substantial property (Wp.18 143M) before reaching the steepest part. Along here (S), there's the chance to catch your breath before beginning to gently climb, rhododendrons to our left, then fork right (Wp.19 151M) to climb more steeply (SW). **Abergavenny** appears surprisingly close down to our left, with **Ysgyryd Fawr** behind us and **Blorenge** immediately in front.

The oak branch 'roof'

On the other side of a wooden gate with a stile to its left, we come to a crossroads (Wp.20 157M). The way ahead looks particularly inviting, but we go right (NW) now climbing more steadily. Extended branches of oak trees from the wood to our left form a roof for our path, the valley we've just climbed out of now to our right. Leaving the woods, the way is sunken between bracken and gorse with some stones underfoot, and has the feeling of past centuries of footsteps before emerging onto open moorland, where we cross a minor path where the surrounding bracken is all blown down.

Sugar Loaf

Before reaching **Deri** ridge we come to a meeting of six ways (Wp.21 165M), and take the wide green path first right, which takes us along the side of the ridge (N). The classic shape of **Sugar Loaf** appears in front of us and we ignore paths to left and right before reaching a track, reinforced for vehicles, that climbs up out of the valley (Wp.22 180M).

Turning left, we climb steadily up towards the corner of a field bounded by a drystone wall and on reaching it, while looking over it back to **Bryn Arw**, marvel at its immaculate construction. Coming to another meeting of the ways (Wp.23 190M), we go slightly left with a pine tree on our right (NW) and head towards the left hand side of a clump of trees which hide the continuing drystone wall. Walking between heather, our path drifts round to the left and we join the path that runs along the top of the ridge before passing beside the National Trust enclosure of **Parc Lodge**. **Sugar Loaf** is now straight ahead. and just as you think this can't be the way, we see an oblique turn to the right (Wp.24 202M NNE).

Although it's now not far back to the car park, it feels like we're miles from anywhere as we head steadily downwards with the path obvious ahead beside our continuing drystone wall, this is another chance to savour the view down the **Vale of Ewyas** that we enjoyed after attaining the ridge of **Bryn Arw**. After turning right at the end of the field, we turn right again at an apology for a cairn (Wp.25 215M), to follow the wall (ESE), initially on the flat, before sweeping left and going steadily down (NW). At a T junction, we turn obliquely right (E) and pass through a kissing gate to the right of a metal gate to reach the car park (Wp.1 226M).

This route starts in the interesting market town of **Crickhowell** which offers the advantage of a choice of refreshment opportunities, and access by public transport. Admittedly, this route entails some road walking, but few good things come without penalties. The name **Crickhowell** is derived from that of the Iron Age fort, **Crug Hywel**, which is set on **Table Mountain** overlooking the town, and is the main objective of the day. But rather than coming straight back down after the ascent, our route continues down the opposite, northern side, sweeps round and down beside **Cuthbert Brook** in **Cwm Cuthbert** and provides an opportunity to stop at the inviting **White Hart** on the **Brecon** road before returning to the town centre.

Access by car:

From **Abergavenny** we take the A40 towards **Brecon**. After passing the town sign for **Crickhowell**, but before reaching its centre, we turn right following car park signs into **Greenhill Way** and immediately left into the pay and display car park.

After leaving the car park (Wp.1 0M) we turn left into **Greenhill Way** (NE) beside neatly tended allotments and immediately see our objective, **Table Mountain**, in front of us. At a mini-roundabout we turn right (ESE) and start climbing steadily with views across the town already opening up over the drystone wall to our right.

At a road junction (Wp.2 5M) we turn left into **Great Oak Road** (N), following a signpost to **Grwynefechan**, and continue climbing steadily with banks on either side but as we pass a line of houses set back to our right the gradient decreases; the view of the town is now to our left with **Table Mountain** straight ahead. After a lane joins us on our left we start climbing steadily again (NE) until, opposite the hum of an electricity sub station, we turn left following a footpath sign through a metal barred gate (Wp.3 16M N).

The tarmac track has grass in the middle and runs between drystone walls entwined with ivy towards **The Wern** farm. Crossing a stile to the left of a metal barred gate, we enter the farmyard and turn right in front of the farmhouse (Wp.4 21M E) to go through another metal barred gate. Following straight across a field; enjoy the flat going as it won't last. At a gate in the opposite corner (Wp.5 24M) we turn left (N) onto a substantial path which turns into a stony sunken lane leading up to a stile to the left of a metal barred gate with a 'Table Mountain' signpost; this is obviously a popular route. Keeping to the right field edge, we cross another stile and then a track and begin to climb more steeply, giving us the excuse to stop and look back at the splendid views over **Crickhowell**. Steep stone steps at the corner of the field lead up to the next stile (Wp.6 33M), where we go left onto a track and over a stile to the right of a metal barred gate.

We follow the right field edge again in the same direction, but at the corner of the next field we go over a stile (Wp.7 38M) and this time head right (E), following waymarks and an ancient hand painted sign in a tree around the back of a farmhouse, up a stony path with straggly woodland to our left and fence to our right. Emerging onto open moorland via a stile to the right of a rusty barred gate (Wp.8 41M), **Table Mountain** is to our left; there's a route directly up it, but we take the more obvious grassy path, straight on between bracken.

Table Mountain seen from Wp.8

Crossing a stream as we make our way around the right of the mountain (NE), we climb steadily with views opening up of **Grwyne Fechan** and the range of mountains beyond, the way flattening out as it runs parallel with a drystone wall. But not for long, because where a path crosses us diagonally (Wp.9 49M), we take a left fork (NW) up towards the bluff. Before reaching it, we fork left again (W) following deep footprints in the turf to climb steeply and swing left (SW), passing between rocks onto the distinct plateau and the cairn at the summit (Wp.10 57M).

The defences of the hill fort are clearly evident and one can easily imagine what an impenetrable fortress it was in its heyday. From the cairn, we head to the other side of the plateau (NNW) and, just to the right of the corner, find a slightly perilous way down. Having successfully negotiated this, we come to a junction of paths (Wp.11 63M). Two come around the mountain, and there's the obvious one ahead, but we take the least obvious path that runs to the left towards a drystone wall and then around to the left (NW) beside it with **Darren Escarpment** in front of us.

The wall is reinforced by a fence in places where it has tumbled down, and we cross several tiny streams that run off the slopes of **Pen Cerrig-calch** before reaching the corner of a field boundary (Wp.12 70M) to find a much larger stream, the formative **Cumbeth Brook**, in a gully. Turning left (SW) we edge between wall and gully until there's a chance to jump the stream and then follow it steeply down between gorse until it begins to drop down even more steeply when we swing away down towards another section of drystone wall.

There are many more streams and attendant boggy patches to cope with before we turn left by another field boundary (S) and drop down yet again to a sheepfold (Wp.13 78M). Here we must avoid the obvious footpath that carries on uphill, and instead find the hand painted footpath sign that beckons us into the sheepfold (E) and through a labyrinth of gates to a green sward between drystone walls and a stream. Turning right (S) we cross it, go along to the left of it, then cross it again to walk along the base of a drystone wall at its edge.

... between walls and a stream ...

After this hopefully not too wet adventure, we emerge into a landscape of open parkland (SE), with burgeoning streams on either side of us and, before long, ford the left hand one (Wp.14 86M).

Ignoring a metal barred gate which would take us up again, we choose the smaller metal gate to its right which takes us down a sunken lane (S) through woodland. Descending steadily, with the water of **Cumbeth Brook** protesting loudly at its downward progress on the other side of a mossy drystone wall, we occasionally glimpse it down between the trees. Then a path goes off to our right over a footbridge (Wp.15 98M) and another to the left, up and over a stile into a field. Leaving the sound of the water, we keep to the edge of the wood, through a wooden gate, and over a stream, suddenly spotting the town across a field; a pub can't be far away! Where there's a choice of metal barred gate to the left and stile to the right (Wp.16 104M) we take the stile which leads us down stone steps and the right hand edge of a field (SW). Over a stile into the next field, we ignore a path down to our right and continue down the right field edge towards the right of a farm building.

Through a paddock, we find a stile none too easily between double gates and donkey stables (Wp.17 113M) and turn right (W) onto a track taking us over a bridge where we can see a beautifully laid out garden with a wooden bridge over the temporarily tamed, **Cumbeth Brook**. On meeting a lane we turn left (SW) to go steeply down to the A40; **The White Hart** is just around the corner to the right (Wp.18 120M). Back along the A40 to **Crickhowell** (SE) and our starting point (Wp.1 132M) is not unpleasant, as there's pavement all the way, and much to see.

Cumbeth Brook

This walk is one of the most gruelling in this book as it is both long and involves significant climbing, but isn't difficult in any other way. It starts with a long hard climb up to **Table Mountain** and then continues upward to **Pen Cerrig-calch** but after that the further two summits of **Pen Allt-mawr** and **Pen Twyn Glas** are of a similar height and the return down the **Grwynne Fawr** valley is downhill all the way. There are spectacular views, particularly from **Pen Cerrig-calch** and although there are no refreshment stops en route, **The Red Lion** in **Llanbedr** is only half a mile from the start.

Access by car:

From **Abergavenny** we take the A40 towards **Brecon**. After passing the town sign for **Crickhowell** but before reaching its centre, turn right following car park signs into 'Greenhill Way' then at a mini-roundabout turn right. Then it's first left signposted 'Grwynne Fawr' to park after a further two miles (3.2km) on the right just passed a right turn signposted 'Llanbedr'.

From our parking space under trees (Wp.1 0M) we continue up the road (N), slightly climbing between high hedges until just past **Ty Mawr Farm** we turn left (Wp.2 6M W) onto a track signposted 'Perth y Pia and Table Mountain'.

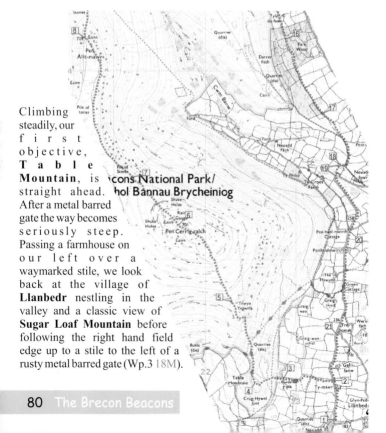

Climbing steadily, our first objective, **Table Mountain**, is straight ahead. After a metal barred gate the way becomes seriously steep. Passing a farmhouse on our left over a waymarked stile, we look back at the village of **Llanbedr** nestling in the valley and a classic view of **Sugar Loaf Mountain** before following the right hand field edge up to a stile to the left of a rusty metal barred gate (Wp.3 18M).

This takes out onto open moorland and a wide grassy path between bracken leads us in the same direction, now breathing deeply. Heading directly up towards the obvious outline of **Table Mountain**, we fork left and cross another path to join Walk 18, up to the cairn that marks the summit (Wp.4 27M). From the cairn we go slightly right towards the far corner of the plateau and find the way down (N) just to its right onto a wide grassy path. First it's down between bracken, soon changes and we're heading steeply up towards the ridge of **Trwyn Ysgwrfa**. Bracken changes to gorse and our path swings first right then left, much easier than the alternative which goes straight up. As the gradient lessens we take a rest to savour the views forward to **Pen y Fan** and **Corn Du** and back to **Ysgyryd Fawr** and **Sugar Loaf** before reaching a division in the paths where we go right (Wp.5 55M NW). Now it's more steadily upwards on a stony path, over a stream and by a path that joins us from the left. After gorse gives way to heather we pass through a wasteland of white stone blocks before reaching the trig point that marks **Pen Cerrig-calch** (Wp.6 68M). This unsung summit has a spectacular three hundred and sixty degree aspect and deserves a long stop, if only to celebrate that nearly all the day's climbing has been done.

After passing to the right of a circular stone shelter, our path can be seen far ahead, swinging to the right on the top of an escarpment. It's gently down at first and we make rapid progress over easy terrain with that elevated feeling that comes when everything around is lower than us. A steep, rocky descent slows us, but then there's grass again underfoot until we meet a neat cairn (Wp.7 85M) after which rocks here and there attempt to stub the toes.

On Pen Allt-mawr (Wp.8)

The view down into **Cwm Banw** with **Sugar Loaf** and **Bryn Arw** in the distance is a picture to behold as we swing right (N) to ascend again to the barren heights of **Pen Allt-mawr** (Wp.8 108M), somewhat softened by the rural landscape to the north. Again, our way is visible far ahead but this time we drop very steeply down from the summit to walk along a ridge on a well-trodden path between bilberries which swings right (NE) with splendid views down both sides

The main path passes left of **Pen Twyn Glas** but we divert onto a minor path to include its summit (Wp.9 139M), our fourth of the day! Here we find what look like a pair of tombstones that are, in fact, the boundary stones of the local estates that historically met here.

Returning to the main path, we continue along a further ridge (N) but now swing left (NW), our way back along the **Grwynne Fawr** valley below to our right clearly visible as an encouragingly distinct green stripe. A shelter just below the ridge on the right (Wp.10 167M) makes a good place to stop and eat a packed lunch before dropping down (N) to the large cairn which marks a major meeting of ways (Wp.11 177M) where we turn sharp right, then right again (SE) to follow a wide green path gently down, half way up the side of the valley. The beginnings of **Grwynne Fechan** are but a trickle below us and conifers on the opposite side stretch to the foot of the valley floor in serried ranks. Meeting an enclosure (Wp.12 202M), we follow its boundary south, constructed of fencing where the original dry stone wall has collapsed. After leaving it, we look out for a smaller path off to the right (Wp.13 212M) which continues along the contour rather than dropping down and crossing the valley to the other side. This looks unpromisingly overgrown to start, but have faith! For a while we push bracken aside, cross a multitude of tiny streams, negotiate a few boggy parts and duck under hawthorns as it staunchly leads us onward in the same direction. Meeting the corner of another dry stone wall enclosure (Wp.14 225M) our path swings a little to the left (SE) until we reach a divide in the ways (Wp.15 240M).

Now it's left to a choice of gate or stile, past a ruined building on our left, through thistles, over a stile to the right of a metal barred gate and on to another ruined building, still between bracken but with a meadow to our right, all in quick succession. Next we cross a stream and go between stinging nettles to a gate that leads into a conifer plantation. The narrow path wends its way through what feels like a secret wood though this impression is quickly destroyed when we reach a wide forest track (Wp.16 253M) even though our path continues on the other side. As woodland changes to meadow on our left, we ignore intriguing mud steps to our right and continue between fence and trees to pass through an area of rosebay willow herb, keeping close to what is now a dry stone wall to leave the wood over a stile (Wp.17 268M). The path is now less distinct, but we continue in the same direction to join another path on the right.

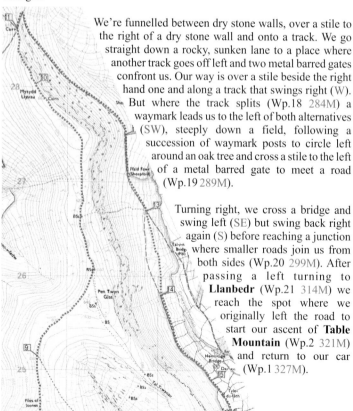

We're funnelled between dry stone walls, over a stile to the right of a dry stone wall and onto a track. We go straight down a rocky, sunken lane to a place where another track goes off left and two metal barred gates confront us. Our way is over a stile beside the right hand one and along a track that swings right (W). But where the track splits (Wp.18 284M) a waymark leads us to the left of both alternatives (SW), steeply down a field, following a succession of waymark posts to circle left around an oak tree and cross a stile to the left of a metal barred gate to meet a road (Wp.19 289M).

Turning right, we cross a bridge and swing left (SE) but swing back right again (S) before reaching a junction where smaller roads join us from both sides (Wp.20 299M). After passing a left turning to **Llanbedr** (Wp.21 314M) we reach the spot where we originally left the road to start our ascent of **Table Mountain** (Wp.2 321M) and return to our car (Wp.1 327M).

At 811 metres, **Waun Fach** is the highest peak in the **Black Mountains** but this is not the reason for this route for, in truth, the peak is not attractive. However, the way up past the Norman castle of **Castell Dinas** onto the sawtooth ridge, sometimes described as 'Dragon's Back', to **Pen y Mallwyn**, coupled with the way down the ridge leading to **Pen Trumau** and thence to **Rhiw Trumau**, with the route constantly circling the delightful **Rhiangoll Valley**, is a walking experience not to be missed. But choose a fine day.

4 | 3H 41M | 7.4 miles/11.8km | 550m / 550m | 3

Access by car:
From **Abergavenny** take the A40 towards **Brecon** but after the town of **Crickhowell** turn right onto the A479 signed 'Talgarth'. Soon after passing the village sign for 'Pengenffordd', arrive at the large car park of **The Castle Inn** on the right (park in the lay-by on the left if not visiting the pub later).

From the pub car park (Wp.1 0M) we make for the far left hand corner and find a signpost to **Castell Dinas** taking us down steps to a track (Wp.2 2M) where we turn right (E). Within fifty metres we hop over a stile on the left and walk along the left hand field edge (NNE), with a series of bumps ahead of us, the so-called 'Dragon's Back', making an inviting prospect for the morning. After a stile, it's slightly to the right (NE) and steeply up the next two fields, still keeping left and ignoring a waymarked stile left. At the top of the second field, somewhat out of breath, we find another stile (Wp.3 13M) and make our way straight up towards the castle ruins ahead. Before reaching a bracken barrier we turn right onto a grassy track (ESE) which takes us more gently up to the right hand corner of the field where we circle to the left (N) and into the castle itself (Wp.4 22M), a Norman construction built on the site of an iron age hill fort. Little stonework remains, but it can claim the prize for highest castle in England and Wales and, to celebrate, you can climb its highest mound chanting 'I'm the King of the Castle' to enjoy the splendid view.

The path threads between what is left of the castle, which we leave to the left of the most substantial and probably more recent building. We drop steeply down (NE) swinging to left and right and thus walking between the remains of ancient ramparts. Our route up the ridge ahead becomes clear before we drop down into a gully to reach a stile (Wp.5 28M). Although a number of paths come together here, we've already established our route up the grassy path in front us between bracken and begin to climb steeply. As it flattens out we can appreciate the disparate views; a patchwork of fields to the left, and grassy, rounded hills and valleys right. After a

... our route up the ridge ...

cairn (Wp.6 39M) it's first gently, then steeply down to **Bwlch Bach a'r Grib** (Wp.7 46M) where a path crosses us before we start ascending the next ridge, where there are paths to left, right and straight up. We take the left (ENE) which first hugs close to the ridge but later moves to the right and runs along the ridge top - great for looking down both sides as long as it's not too windy. Further on, there's a similar set of choices and this time we make a point of climbing along the ridge's crest even though the path on the right would be easier. Passing a cairn built to help walkers find their way down the ridge in poor visibility (Wp.8 59M), it's clear how dangerous losing your way coming down here could be.

The magnificent cairn at Wp.9

The next cairn is truly magnificent (Wp.9 64M) and marks leaving the plateau above to find the ridge; at last the series of steep climbs is over. Forking right shortly after the cairn onto a minor path we now climb steadily, continuing in the same direction. At the top we meet a major path and turn right (Wp.10 86M SSE) to walk across an open and windswept area of moorland to a cairn that indicates the inauspicious peak of **Pen y Mallwyn** (Wp.11 89M). We can now see the flat top of **Waun Fach** and our way ahead along a wide ridge (SE). The three ridges of the **Black Mountains** are all visible on the left, with innumerable bumps of differing sizes to the right, though there are no views into the valleys.

Our way is along the flat and then only slightly uphill to the summit of **Waun Fach** (Wp.12 119M), unceremoniously marked by the concrete base of a removed trig point surrounded by an area of churned up mud. Doesn't it deserve better?

The path onward to **Pen y Gadair Fawr** - visited on 'Walk 10, Mynydd Du' - is obvious, ours is not. But moving away from the trig point base to the right (WSW) we find it. This is a good place for a picnic lunch; our way will literally be all downhill from here. After our repast it's steadily down a boggy path over moorland grass with the way ahead obvious, swinging to the left and along a ridge. Now you'll see why the series of ridges climbed this morning (to our right) are called the 'Dragon's Back' and also why we found them so arduous.

An isolated cairn (Wp.13 136M) shows us the way onto the ridge and we keep to its centre rather than taking the little path to the left. To our right the black, volcanic soil is so thin that only a few odd tussocks of grass can maintain a foothold; somehow disturbing surroundings. Then after passing the cairn that marks **Pen Trumau** we drift to the left (S) to line up with another ridge even though we won't be venturing onto it. First it's only steadily down but suddenly the way becomes very steep, only flattening just before we reach a cairn where several paths meet (Wp.14 154M).

Our way is sharp right (WNW) down the right hand side of the valley ahead, ignoring the smaller path even further to the right that follows the contour. It's steadily down to start with, becoming steeper as we cross the acclivity of **Rhiw Trumau**.

... the path becomes a rocky track ...

Scattered farms in the valley have an idealised, rural look about them as the path becomes a rocky track and we head back towards the hill fort. Through a metal barred gate by some sheep pens (Wp.15 184M), we leave the moorland landscape and the track bends to the left (W). It's still rocky though and many of the rocks are loose, making the going uncertain.

After two more gates we arrive in a wide, fenced in area before another gate takes us down into a sunken lane which runs between holly trees. At last the speed of descent lessens and we meet a road (Wp.16 195M) where we turn right (NW) but it almost immediately swings left (WNW). Now we enjoy perambulating gently down between beech hedges, walking in the middle of the road as nettles are attempting to sting us from both sides and there's not a wheeled vehicle to be seen.

Passing **Cwmfforest Riding Centre** we cross a stream and the road swings left but returns to its original direction before taking a hairpin left (Wp.17 206M) at which point we go straight on (NW) along a muddy track which dries out and becomes stony after we've negotiated a stream using stepping stones.

After crossing another track with gates both sides and ignoring a further track on the left, we pass farm buildings on the right and rejoin our outward route, noticing the steps up on our left (Wp.2 219M) that lead to the car park (Wp.1 221M) and a welcoming pint at **The Castle**.

21 LLANGATTOCK

This route starts along the tranquil **Monmouthshire and Brecon Canal**, above the village of **Llangattock**, with views of the impressive limestone escarpment that forms the northern edge of **Mynydd Llangatwg**, then via field paths beside woodland to the dramatic world of the **Craig y Cilau Nature Reserve** where it runs along the base of the escarpment and up a ridge to look over **Llangattock** and **Crickhowell** to **Table Mountain** before returning to the village. A visit to the bar of **The Old Rectory Hotel** provides a satisfying end to this adventure.

Access by car:
From **Abergavenny** we take the A40 towards **Brecon**. After passing through the centre of **Crickhowell**, we turn left onto the A4077 signed **Gilwern**, left at the traffic lights on the far side of the bridge over the **Usk**, and then immediately right towards **Llangattock**. In the village we turn right into a lane signed 'Dardy' and go round to the left in front of the church and left again into the modern residential development of **Church View** to find the car park.

From the car park (Wp.1 0M) we go through the hole in the wall towards the church. Turning left, are immediately confronted with a choice of lanes signed 'Dardy' to right and 'Ffawyddog' to left. Our way is left, past **The Old Rectory Hotel** set back behind lawns to our right; if you're already thinking ahead to lunch, they do bar meals.

After leaving the village (W), the lane climbs steeply but flattens just before we reach a bridge over the **Monmouthshire and Brecon Canal** (Wp.2 6M); it seems odd, somehow, that we have climbed <u>up</u> to reach it.

Table Mountain

Turning left and walking along the well-maintained towpath (S), **Darren Cilau** is prominent on the right while **Crickhowell** and the immediately recognisable outline of **Table Mountain** is on the left.

After the canal swings right then left we go under a bridge (Wp.3 17M), turn left up from the towpath to the road and left again onto it (WSW) passing **The Canal House** and **Llangattock Boat Club** on our right before beginning gently uphill. At a footpath sign on the right (Wp.4 20M) we go over a stile and straight across a field (W) to a stile on the opposite side and follow the right field edge towards **Cilau Farm**, enjoying magnificent views all along the

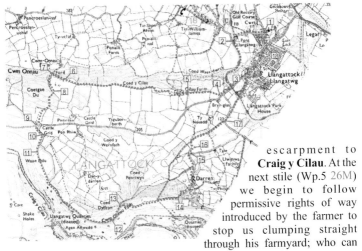

escarpment to **Craig y Cilau**. At the next stile (Wp.5 26M) we begin to follow permissive rights of way introduced by the farmer to stop us clumping straight through his farmyard; who can blame him! These go left onto a track then immediately right up stone steps hidden in a hedge to a stile, across a field.

At the end of farm buildings we go over another stile and right (N) by a fence, to join the original route of the footpath at a signpost that directs us left to **Cwm Onnau**. Here, the way is a track which we follow across a field (W) until it joins woodland on the right.

We clamber over a succession of stiles, with woods dropping down to a valley on our right and fields drifting up towards the mountains on our left, until suddenly, after a stile to the right of a gate, the way disappears. However, keeping along the right hand edge of the field and avoiding dropping down to the right towards the water (now audible), we come to a feeding trough (Wp. 6 47M) where we find a waypoint sign on a post and follow the direction of its arrow to go down a track to meet a river (Wp.7 51M).

Here, we turn sharp left (S) to climb steeply out of the valley, following the edge of a wood, but where it bends to the left and there is a grassy clearing with a plethora of molehills (Wp.8 59M) turn right (SW) into it and find a stony track through it that exits the wood via a rusty metal barred gate. Initially we head diagonally right across the field in front of us around some trees but then go straight up and over a stile to a steep bank and a road (Wp.9 69M).

Guided by a signpost, we cross the road and follow a track (SE) that is initially tarmacked but just in front of a gate (Wp.10 78M) turn right (SW) along a field edge. Ahead we can see the line of the escarpment; our objective is to walk along the base of it. Leaving the field boundary we drop steeply down towards a flat boggy area but on reaching it (Wp.11 87M) ignore the path that crosses it instead making our way to the right around its edge (SSE). The indistinct path takes us through woodland and over large rocks to rejoin the path that came across the bog (SE) and is now well defined.

After following a dry stone wall reinforced by trees, the way goes down again into what feels like a hidden valley with scree up to our right and following a fence on our left which is the boundary of woodland we swing gently around to the left (E) ignoring any paths on our right. After passing an enormous boulder (Wp.12 107M NE) and a stream, the upper reaches of **Nant Onneau** joins us and we fork right (Wp.13 112M) away from it to climb steadily (E) up the ridge.

What a place to stop!

In what seems a short time, the stream is far below us in the valley and here the way is slightly precipitous, but then we reach a delightful promontory with a judiciously positioned bench with views of **Llangattock** with **Crickhowell** beyond and **Table Mountain** above that. What a place to stop!

Conifers hang above our path before we meet a lane (Wp.14 125M) where we turn left (ENE), go over a cattle grid and first steadily then steeply down (N). Immediately after a right hand hairpin we go over a stile to our left (Wp.15 135M) and cross a field to encounter **Nant Onneau** again.

Finding no place to comfortably cross, we follow the footprints of earlier walkers to the right along the bank and find a crude stone bridge (Wp.16 139M) to cross the next field to a metal gate. Ignoring the path that goes diagonally up across a field we turn right (ENE) and follow a track beside a fence, go through a gate and swing right to cross a stile to the right of a gate back onto the lane (Wp.17 148M).

Turning left (NE), we make our way back to the village, crossing the canal before reaching its centre where we turn left (Wp.18 159M N) signed 'Dardy', go over a bridge and walk between cottages back to the church, through the hole in the wall and to the car park (Wp.1 161M).

This route ascends **Tor y Foel** from **Llangynidr**, a significant climb but one which demonstrates that summits don't have to be that high to provide magnificent vistas all around. Then it drops steeply down towards **Talybont Reservoir** but turns before reaching it to drop gently down across farmland, to the **Monmouthshire and Brecon Canal** and a relaxed stroll back. **The Coach and Horses**, by our starting point, is very popular, and with good reason.

| 3 | 2H 44M | 5.4 miles/8.6km | | 425m / 425m | | 3* |

* 5 for longer alternative

Access by car:
Coming from **Brecon**, head towards **Abergavenny** on the A40 and, shortly after leaving the town, turn off the dual carriageway onto the B4558 which runs alongside the **Monmouthshire and Brecon Canal**. After **Talybont-on-Usk** head for **Llangynidr** but before reaching the village centre, where the main road bends sharp right over a bridge, go straight on signed **Bwlch** and almost immediately park on the right by a canal lock.

> **Longer Version**
> (Combines elements of Walks 22 and 23) At Wp.8, find the footpath to the left of the cattle grid and cross the fields to join the **Brinore Tramroad** back to **Talybont-on-Usk** (Wp.1 to Wp.6 of route 22 reversed), then follow the canal back to **Llangynidr** rejoining at Wp.12 (Wp.10 back to Wp.1 of route 22 reversed). It has the significant advantage of providing refreshment stops en route.

View from the towpath near the walk's start

From the lock (Wp.1 0M), we walk to the right (SW) along the canal towpath, with **The Coach and Horses'** lawns stretching down to the canal on the other side, before we go under the road bridge.

The lock crossing at Wp.2

The canal sweeps around to the right (W) with the road accompanying it, while **Afon Crawnon** tumbles beneath both to join the **River Usk** just down the valley. At the next lock (Wp.2 7M), we cross the lock itself to follow a waymarked path steeply up into a wood (SW).

After a stile, the way flattens and we can see our objective, **Tor y Foel**, through trees to our right as we walk along a pleasant path with the sound of **Afon Crawnon** bubbling below to our left. Passing from the wood into a field, we make for a stile in the opposite hedge (Wp.3 14M) where we turn right up the field edge (W) and start to steadily climb.

Over the next stile and to the left of a water trough (following helpful yellow waymarks), we hug the left hand field edge with the summit directly ahead. After passing through a metal barred gate, we cross a track and continue up the right hand field edge to an unusual stile where we have to heave ourselves onto a huge chunk of rock before we can get over it and continue following the right hand field edge.

For the first time the way isn't obvious, but heading towards the farmhouse and just to its right, we find a track that passes to the left of the other house which is a little further back. At the top of the track (Wp.4 29M) we cross a lane and follow a bridleway sign through a wooden gate to the left of a metal barred gate and continue to climb steadily.

Further on, the way becomes a stony sunken lane between hawthorns, and after we pass through a wooden gate, views of the valley to our left and **Mynydd Llangynidr** open up.

When we reach a stile to the left of a metal barred gate (Wp.5 44M) which takes us though onto open moorland, it seems the right time for a long stop to savour the delights of where we've got to, and to recognize the effort we've put into it. Looking back from our perch on the stile, there are beautiful views down the **Usk Valley** with **Table Mountain** and **Sugar Loaf** on the left and **Craig y Castell** and **Blorenge** on the right.

The way is now a grassy path between bracken, as it passes a conifer plantation and crosses another path just after leaving the plantation's shadow. As the **Usk Valley** begins to open up in the other direction, we climb steeply for the first time. You might think we're about to reach the summit, but find it's a false one and there's another hump to climb. This happens twice before the going flattens, now between heather, and we pass a pond to eventually reach the cairn at the summit (Wp.6 73M) and magnificent views in all directions.

Turning to our right, we drop down steeply (NNW) between tussocky grass with **Talybont Reservoir** on our left (see photo on the next page). grateful that this was not our way up. Although not marked on the 1:25000 OS map, this is a distinct, well used path which takes us down to a mountain road (Wp.7 98M) where we turn right (NE) along it to continue steadily downwards in the direction of **Allt yr Esgair**.

Talybont Reservoir as seen on the steep descent

At a bridleway sign to the left of the road, just before reaching a cattle grid (Wp.8 102M) we go obliquely right (S) up a track across moorland which climbs the hill. But not for long, as we come to a fork (Wp.9 105M) and take the left option (E) which takes us gently down over a stile to the right of a rusty barred gate into a field.

The way continues down, following an obvious path across a stream, through a gate and a small conifer plantation down to a metal barred gate at the bottom left hand corner of a field (Wp.10 117M).

Passing along the bottom of the next field (SE), we cross another stream, ignore a farm track that crosses us, and duck beneath an overgrown hawthorn hedge beside us before the view of the **River Usk** and **Monmouthshire and Brecon Canal** running close together below us opens up. A succession of streams crossed, stiles clambered over and gates passed through continue to take us gently down in the same direction, until we pass between two copses and follow a bridleway sign across a flatter field with the canal now close on our left. After heading straight across it, we jump a stream by an ancient tree and use a choice of gate or stile to pass into woodland (Wp.11 126M). Before long, a wooden barred gate takes us out onto a track and left to a girder bridge over the canal (Wp.12 133M) and an opportunity to pause and gaze at the serene progress of any passing narrow boats.

On the other side of the bridge we cross a stile to our right, go down some steps and turn left onto a well maintained towpath (SE). Opposite a picture-book white cottage we rest on a bench carefully positioned to watch the world go by (Wp.13 148M) before following the towpath (E) passed a staircase of three locks, at the bottom of which we join our outward route back to our start. **The Coach and Horses**, with its canalside lawns, is recommended for lunch.

The picture-book white cottage

The Brecon Beacons **91**

One of the easiest walks in this book. Why? Because it's only five miles, has no steep gradients and is simple to follow. We follow the old **Brinore Tramroad**, which ran all the way down to **Talybont-on-Usk** from **Tredegar**, with views over **Talybont Reservoir** across to the eastern end of the **Brecon Beacons**, then drop down through farmland to return along the towpath of the **Monmouthshire and Brecon Canal**. There are two pubs on the route; **The White Hart** at the start/end provides traditional pub grub, whilst **The Traveller's Rest** just before the end, has a more upmarket restaurant.

Access by car:
Coming from **Brecon**, head towards **Abergavenny** on the A40 and, shortly after leaving the town, turn off the dual carriageway onto the B4558 which runs alongside the **Momouthshire and Brecon Canal** to **Talybont-on-Usk**. Park in the car park of **The White Hart** at the far end of the village if you intend to imbibe there later; alternatively, there's plenty of space to park elsewhere in the village.

Behind **The White Hart** (Wp.1 0M), we ignore the 'Route for Walkers' sign to cross a bridge over the canal, following instead the 'Taff Trail' sign to turn right up a muddy track (SW). After passing a post on the left with a plethora of waymark symbols for both walkers and riders, the track swings left onto a bridge over the dismantled Merthyr to Brecon Railway, then right where we notice what looks like a tombstone informing us that the **Brinore Tramroad** was opened in 1851; notice the stones in the middle of the track that once held supports for the tramroad's rails.

Ahead looms the summit of **Tor y Foel**. Passing through a gate (Wp.2 11M), we continue to climb up the steady gentle incline that the tramroad dictated, and ignore both a path down to our right and a path with a blue arrow waymark climbing steeply up into woods to our left (Wp.3 18M). After **Talybont Reservoir** appears ahead we enter the woods (S) we've been walking beside, and a path crosses us diagonally (Wp.4 25M). The **Taff Trail** which we've been following so far goes down to the right here, but we carry straight on to follow the **Brinore Tramroad** and the signpost to 'Trefil'. The reservoir is now clearly visible though the trees, but just before reaching a gate, we go over a stile to our left (Wp.5 38M) and turn obliquely back on ourselves (NE) across a field and away from it.

After passing through a gap in the hedge into the next field, we climb steadily making for the solitary tree in the middle of it to find a waymark on a post, then heading slightly to the right towards a waymarked stile, crossing a stream before we reach it.

Talybont Reservoir

After the stile we go slightly to the right again, and at the top of the field can look back to enjoy the view across **Talybont Reservoir** and forward down the **Usk Valley** as far as **Sugar Loaf**. Although there's no obvious path here, we carry on confidently and down the other side of the hill find a stile a little to the right of a metal barred gate which takes us onto a mountain road (Wp.6 49M).

Immediately to our left there's a cattle grid, but we turn right (SSW) up the road and then follow a bridleway sign left (S) up a track across moorland which climbs the hill. But not for long, as at a fork (Wp.7 51M) we take the left option (E) which takes us gently down over a stile to the right of a rusty barred gate into a field. The way continues down following an obvious path across a stream, through a gate and a small conifer plantation down to a metal barred gate at the bottom left hand corner of a field (Wp.8 69M).

The river and canal running close together

Passing along the bottom of the next field (SE) we cross another stream, ignore a farm track that crosses us and duck beneath an overgrown hawthorn hedge beside us before the view of the **River Usk** and **Monmouthshire and Brecon Canal** running close together below us opens up.

A succession of streams crossed, stiles clambered over and gates passed through continue to take us gently down in the same direction until we pass between two copses and follow a bridleway sign across a flatter field with the canal now close on our left. After heading straight across it, we jump a stream by an ancient tree and use a choice of gate or stile to pass into woodland (Wp.9 90M).

Before long a wooden barred gate takes us out onto a track and left to a girder bridge over the canal (Wp.10 93M) and an opportunity to pause and gaze at the serene progress of any passing narrow boats.

On the other side of the bridge we cross a stile to our right, go down steps and turn right onto a well maintained towpath to pass beneath it.

The towpath provides easy walking (NW), with the canal's banks bedecked with primroses and celandines, running close to the old road between **Abergavenny** and **Brecon**.

The towpath after Wp.10

Where the canal goes into the 343 metre long **Ashford Tunnel** (Wp.11 119M) there is no towpath, so horses were led over the top while men 'legged' the boats through the tunnel lying on their backs, an experience that we can recommend trying first hand on the canal that runs through the **Black Country Museum** in the West Midlands. We also go over the top, following the road, but via a stile into a field to walk the other side of a hedge from it. After the canal emerges from the tunnel, we walk beside the road until it drops down for us to continue walking along the towpath.

The Traveller's Rest (Wp.12 136M) has a garden that backs onto the canal and straight after, we encounter a series of attractive cottages whose front doors open onto it.

Then after a bridge, located somewhat incongruously by the canal, we find a truck from the **Brimore Tramroad** complete with an interesting information board. We were intrigued to learn that the only way an upbound driver knew when a truck was on its way down and therefore to turn into one of the passing places, was by the sound of the descending driver clanging on its side with a piece of metal!

The Brimore Tramroad truck

Not long after, we arrive back at **The White Hart** (Wp.1 147M).

Starting from the **Storey Arms Centre**, this route explores the opposite side of the valley from the more popular ascent of **Corn Du** and **Pen y Fan** (Route 27). It starts down the old drovers' track towards **Brecon** before crossing the valley to enter the **Craig Cerrig-gleisand Nature Reserve**, and encompasses the summits of both **Fan Frynach** and **Fan Fawr**. Although there is no path shown on the Ordnance Survey map across the moorland between the two, there is a well-trodden way.

*Burger Bar in lay-by opposite **Storey Arms Centre**.

Access by car:
From **Merthyr Tydfil**, take the A470 towards **Brecon**. Eight miles north of the roundabout with the A465 Heads of the Valley road, and soon after passing a large car park at **Pont ar Daf** on the right, reach the **Storey Arms Centre**. Disappointingly, this is not a pub but an Outdoor Activity Centre but can be identified by the red telephone box outside and the large lay-by on the opposite side of the road where we park. From **Brecon**, we take the A470 towards **Merthyr Tydfil**; the **Storey Arms Centre** is seven miles to the south.

Crossing the road from the lay-by to the telephone box (Wp.1 0M), we take the track signed **Taff Trail** which runs almost parallel to the road (NW). Descending gently, we pass through a kissing gate to the left of an old wooden gate, and the fence to our right is replaced by a well-constructed drystone wall (N). The way becomes steeper and departs further from the road, which is now on the other side of the valley, and we pass through a wooden gate (Wp.2 16M) to enter the National Trust property of **Blaenglyn Farm**. We cross a substantial bridge, appropriate for four wheel drive vehicles (a reminder that this was once the main turnpike used by stage coaches between **Brecon** and **Merthyr Tydfil**) and just before another bridge, we turn left over a stile to the right of a five-barred gate (Wp.3 27M), following a signpost to 'Llwyn-y-celyn Youth Hostel'. We head towards and across a stile on the other side of the field (SW), and then go left along a muddy track, hearing the sound of water before coming to a wooden bridge (Wp.4 30M).

There's no discernible path on the other side, but we head straight up the field (W) towards two isolated trees. Further up and slightly to the left is a signpost beside a stone stile (Wp.5 39M), on the other side of which is a lay-by off the main road.

Crossing the road to another lay-by with a well maintained picnic site, we go through a

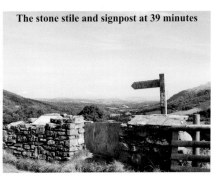

The stone stile and signpost at 39 minutes

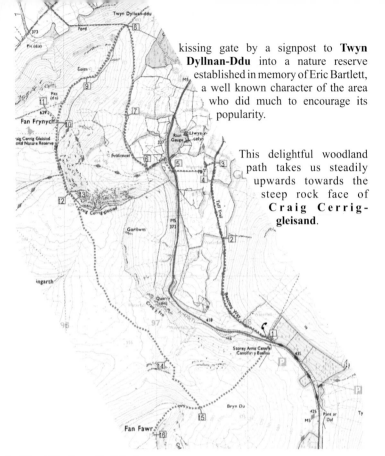

kissing gate by a signpost to **Twyn Dyllnan-Ddu** into a nature reserve established in memory of Eric Bartlett, a well known character of the area who did much to encourage its popularity.

This delightful woodland path takes us steadily upwards towards the steep rock face of **Craig Cerrig-gleisand**.

The slit in the wall at Wp.6

Reaching a wooden five-barred gate, we squeeze through a slit in the wall to its left (Wp.6 49M) to stumble across a tourist sign board; unusual to find one so far from the road! Taking a track to the right (NW), we continue to climb, but soon the way becomes a path across moorland. We cross a stream on stepping stones, meet a gate with no fence attached either side, and cross another stream down in a ravine (Wp.7 62M) before a crossroad of tracks (Wp.8 77M).

We take the one to the left (SW) and go uphill, slightly diagonally back on ourselves, towards a rounded knoll. The track runs steeply up between fences on both sides to reach a barred gate with a stile; going through it rather than over the stile might be a good idea if you're running short of breath!

A large rock to our left (Wp.9 89M) provides a welcome spot for a rest, though our way, thankfully, is flatter again.

We're now in open moorland but still on a substantial track, and a little to our right is **Fan Frynach**, an unassuming bump rising between the surrounding moorland. On the map there is an obvious path to it, so we ignore the paths running between the heather until we reach it (Wp.10 97M). It takes us diagonally backwards (NW) to the trig point (Wp.11 101M).

Open moorland after Wp.9

Returning to the track, we continue (S) towards our second peak of the day, **Fan Fawr**, the classic squared wire fence topped by a single strand of barb strung between wooden posts on our left. The dark cliff of **Craig Cerrig-gleisand** is now in front of us and to our left - it's now obvious why we didn't come straight up here from the road. Descending for a change, we pass a pond on our right to reach a rusty barred gate and go over a stile to its right (Wp.12 117M). Another stile over the fence to our left leads to an obvious path which runs along the other side of the fence near the cliff edge, but we carry on up the field parallel to this path (SE) although there's no discernible path. At the top of the field, **Fan Fawr** is obvious ahead (Wp.13 120M) and though not marked on the map, a reasonably well-defined path heads in that direction, towards the middle of the **Fan Fawr** barrow at first, then bearing increasingly left as we approach it until we can see our starting point, the **Storey Arms Centre**, straight ahead.

Stepping stones across a little stream (Wp.14 145M) mark the start of a boggy area where the path becomes indistinct, but keeping to the higher ground and following the contour around **Fan Fawr**, we meet the larger path (Wp.15 154M) which runs directly up from the **Storey Arms Centre**. Turning right (W), we climb ever more steeply until we reach the plateau and thence make our way to the cairn that marks the summit (Wp.16 178M). Weirdly, the trig point which we can see at the other end of the barrow is not the summit, and the views from there are not as good as from here so what's the point of trudging there and back?

Instead, we return the way we've just come (NE), this time keeping to the larger path. The route always descends but undulates, so that sometimes we can see our destination and sometimes not, though the scar on the other side of the valley which marks the well-trodden path from it up towards **Pen y Fan** is always ahead and confirms our route. Apparently, the burger bar in the lay-by opposite the **Storey Arms Centre (Wp.1** 207M) is open every day of the year!

Although much less walked, this is my favourite ascent of **Pen y Fan** - less walked no doubt, because the start is a little tricky to find. The route follows the valley of **Cwm Llwch** to look down on the mountain pool **Llyn Cwm Llwch** before ascending to the distinctive, flat summit of **Corn Du**, then on to **Pen y Fan** and a short clamber down onto the ridge of **Cefn Cwm Llwch** before dropping steadily down with stunning views of **Brecon** and its environs to return along quiet lanes to the start.

Access by car:

From **Brecon** Town Centre, cross the bridge over the **River Usk** on the B4601 and take the second significant turning on the left **Ffrwdgrech Road**, opposite the **Drover's Arms**. There is a signpost to the **Taff Trail** here but it's too small to be reliably seen from a car. After driving under the A40 bypass the road splits into three; take the middle one, then at a crossroads go ahead into the narrowest of lanes to eventually reach a metal barred gate. Passing through it, the car park is on the grass to the left, a beautiful green space interspersed with ancient oaks bounded by a track and a sparkling river. Few seem to find this idyllic spot.

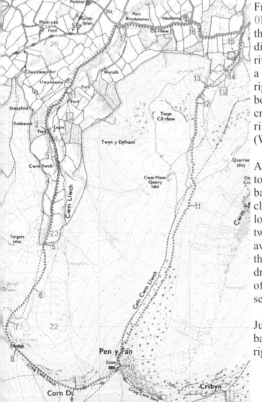

From the car park (Wp.1 0M), we continue along the track in the same direction (SW) with the river on our left. Ignoring a smaller track to the right, the way becomes boulder-strewn before we cross a tributary of 'our' river on a footbridge (Wp.2 8M).

After climbing over a stile to the left of a metal barred gate, the track climbs (S) so that we now look down at the river twinkling below. Veering away from the river, with the track passing between drystone walls, the range of mountains in front of us seems almost menacing.

Just before reaching a barred gate, we pass to the right of some hawthorns following a sign instructing us to keep to the waymarked path (Wp.3 12M). Clearly, we are being diverted around a farmhouse that is being restored. After two stiles we return to the route of the original path that went through the farmyard (Wp.4 16M) and begin to climb. The way is green and grassy, swinging to right and left on a ridge between two valleys with rows of trees that have clearly suffered from the elements. Over another stile we continue to climb up a wide grassy path and ignoring a smaller path to our right we reach a stile which takes us into the National Trust property of **Cwm Llwch** (Wp.5 28M).

The way now becomes awkwardly stony so that we have to be careful where we put our feet as we continue plodding upward. Reaching a cairn (Wp.6 38M), we take the right fork (SW) which is initially a grassy track but reverts quickly back to stones as it goes up to join the ridge between **Corn Du** and **Pen Milan**. The left fork at the cairn goes down to the glacial pool of **Llyn Cwm Llwch**, which according to local tradition is bottomless.

... a beautifully laid pavement ...

For the energetic, this can make an interesting diversion as an even steeper path - let's call it a scramble - goes up from the pool to join our route a little further on. Attaining the **Craig Cwm Llwch** ridge (Wp.7 52M), we turn left (SE) and are buffeted by the wind which always seems to be blowing a gale here whatever the conditions are in the valley. Passing the obelisk in memory of Tommy Jones (Wp.8 59M), whose story is related in **Pen y Fan from Pont ar Daf**, Walk 27, we ascend gradually on a beautifully laid pavement and then quite steeply for the last section to the flat topped summit of **Corn Du** (Wp.9 81M).

Crossing (NE) to **Pen y Fan** (Wp.10 100M), with the popular way up from **Pont ar Daf** joining us like a motorway, we add a rock to the enormous cairn and go behind it to find our way down via **Cefn Cwm Llwch** (N). This is initially a steep path which we have to clamber down with a dangerous drop to the right but steadily becomes easier down the ridge (NE). The way is rocky, but here and there drainage channels and a pavement have been laid to prevent erosion and make our going easier. We were just remarking on how well trod the way was when part of the reason overtook us in the form of twenty youngsters in combat fatigues on an exercise from the military base in the valley.

Looking eastwards from Pen y Fan

As the ridge broadens there is the option to walk beside the path on the tussocky grass, a choice we found easier. Ahead is a minor peak and it feels like we're going slightly up to it but maybe this is an illusion after travelling downward for so long.

Reaching it (Wp.11 140M), we are presented with a semicircle of four hillocks ahead of us; our way is down the valley between the two to our right, **Cwm Gdiw**. From the peak we can walk either on the grassy top of the ridge (our choice) or on the muddy path that clings a little way down the right hand side of the ridge. Either way, we must eventually use the muddy path which continues to take us down, passing a grassy path that goes off to our right towards **Allt Ddu**.

The city of **Brecon** is directly ahead, and you'll be amazed at how small it is from here, the only city smaller that I can think of is **St David's**. A large, flat topped rock just to the right of the path provides us with an ideal vantage point to survey the valley, classically U-shaped with the beginnings of a river creating a V-shaped notch in its bottom. The burgeoning river is fed by a myriad of streams which we cross, the way being rocky again. As the path flattens out and becomes grassy between bracken at the lower altitude, we fork right (Wp.12 166M) and make towards a wooden barred gate with a stile to its right where there's a National Trust sign (Wp.13 171M). Crossing to the opposite corner of the marshy field, you're likely to see cars parked on the other side of a gate (Wp.14 177M) and the start of a narrow lane.

Passing a bigger car park, tastefully enclosed by young trees, we carry on down the narrow lane, crossing a cattle grid until we reach a crossroads (Wp.15 185M). Here we are confronted by massive white-on-red signs both sides of the road indicating no entry to military vehicles, so large that we can only guess that they're for tank drivers of tanks with severely limited vision! We turn left (W) up another quiet lane and reach a T junction (Wp.16 200M) and turn left again to continue between well tended hedges, passing a somewhat out of place modern farmhouse.

Crossing a bridge, we look over to our right at the water tumbling over rocks worn into a beautiful formation that looks like it has been designed. At the next crossroads (Wp.17 212M) we turn left (SW) into an even narrower lane which returns us to the car park (Wp.1 222M).

As with **Sugar Loaf Mountain**, no excuses are made for there being three routes in this book that climb **Pen y Fan** and its near neighbour **Corn Du**, for they are the highest and most frequently visited of all the summits in the **Brecon Beacons**. This route approaches them from the south and caps the other two by including **Cribyn** as well. Starting at the farthest point that the road that runs beside **Pontsticill Reservoir** reaches, it crosses the dam of the now disused **Lower Neuadd Reservoir** and climbs up onto the ridge of **Graig Fan Ddu**, then traverses the series of ridges that join the three celebrated peaks before returning gently down an ancient track.

Access by car:

From the roundabout where the A470 crosses the A465 just north of **Merthyr Tydfil**, head east on the A465 towards **Abergavenny**. Leaving at the first junction, go right and almost immediately left across the A4054 onto a minor road that winds along the three miles to **Pontsticill**. Keeping left through the village, the **Pontsticill Reservoir** appears on your right and after a further one and a half miles, turn left then ignore a turn on the right signed **Talybont**. After passing a car park signed 'Taff Fechan', leave your car at the side of the road by a conifer plantation just before a prominent track forks to the right. A signpost which points to 'Taff Trail' in two directions, 'Neuadd and Bwlch ar y Fan' in the others, confirms you're in the right place.

From the roadside (Wp.1 0M) we continue on the road (NNW) passing a green barrier and a 'No Vehicular Traffic' sign, with **Pen y Fan** and **Corn Du** rising up in front of us and **Cribyn** a little to our right. Today's three objectives are already clearly in view - what an exciting prospect!

After passing through a gate beside a cattle grid (Wp.2 10M) we turn left to follow a path (W) that zigzags down to the derelict workings of the **Lower Neuadd Reservoir**. Reaching its dam via a neat bridge, we stop to savour the view, which has a picture postcard quality before crossing it to a metal barred gate (Wp.3 18M).

The picture postcard Lower Neuadd Reservoir

Here we take the left of the two paths climbing up onto the **Graig Fan Ddu** ridge that confront us; the right one is more direct but the final clamber is more severe and the stunning views to be enjoyed while walking along the ridge would be missed by going this way. Our way is initially down and across a gully but then it's increasingly steeply up to the right of a conifer plantation. The views back all along the valley of the **Upper Neuadd**, **Lower Neuadd**, **Pentwyn** and **Pontsticill Reservoirs** with the various forests that encapsulate them are more than enough excuse for the many stops we make. Arriving breathless at the top of the ridge we turn right (Wp.4 41M NW) to follow a well-defined path that runs close to the edge of the escarpment.

Our way is now along a series of ridges which take us gently upwards almost all the way to the peaks. There are continuing, fantastic views to the right but we find it best to pause to enjoy them and concentrate on where we put our feet while moving. Passing a cairn (Wp.5 52M) that marks where the more direct route up the ridge joins us we look back and it seems as though the whole world is spread out in front of us. The path is now very close to the right hand edge so we can't see into the valley to our left, but as we progress it becomes rockier and where the ridge narrows views are revealed into the narrow, rarely visited valley of **Cwm Crew**.

... strange striations ...

For a short while we cross rocks that exhibit strange striations as if scored by prehistoric sleds. At the end of the ridge (Wp.6 99M), somewhat surreally, we can see cars parked way, way down to our left on the main **Merthyr Tydfil** to **Brecon** road. Dropping down (NNE) to **Bwlch Duwynt** (Wp.7 105M) where the path from **Pont ar Daf** snakes up to meet us, we go straight across the wide cross-roads to ascend the exquisitely laid pavement and climb over giant rock steps before reaching the summit of **Corn Du** (Wp.8 110M). The serene patchwork of fields to the north contrasts starkly with the beautiful, cruel peaks that surround us.

Carefully descending to our right (ENE) it's but a hop, skip and a jump up the wide path to our second summit of **Pen y Fan** (Wp.9 121M) and its giant cairn which provides a necessary windbreak for a lunch stop. The views from here are particularly grand and, on a clear day, **Cadair Idris** can be seen to the north, **Exmoor** to the south.

Turning right (SE) and crossing the plateau, we head towards its far corner in the direction of the **Neuadd Reservoirs** and can see our way steeply down to the left and up the other side of the valley to **Cribyn**. We go very carefully down over rocks to start, with a vertiginous drop to our left, then follow a zigzagging laid pavement that takes us very steeply down before choosing the grass to the left of the stony path for the remainder, as it's less slippery.

Sophisticated stepping stones.

Nearing the bottom, we ignore a path that goes off right (Wp.10 137M), then cross a sophisticated set of stepping stones over a pond to climb up (ENE) another laid pavement to **Cribyn** (Wp.11 155M). You have to take your hat off to the Brecon Beacons National Park Authority for the quality of these pavements which admirably solve the difficult problem of protecting the environment while not spoiling it in the process.

From here we can look back at **Pen y Fan** and see it, perhaps, at its best and forward along a series of bluffs culminating in **Hay Bluff** itself.

Turning right at the cairn (S), it's steadily down with a steep drop to our left, swinging slowly around to the left down **Craig Cwm Cynwyn**.

Bizarrely, if you're carrying binoculars, you can perhaps see your parked car from here, even though it's several miles away, such is the view down the valley to the series of reservoirs and **Taf Fechan Forest**.

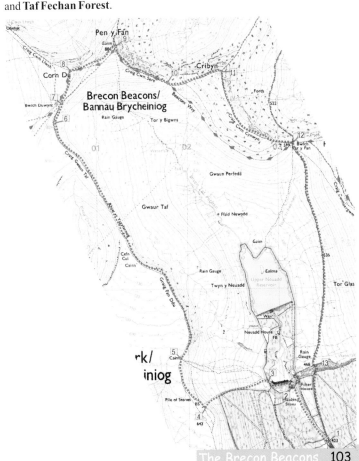

Pen y Fan

Ahead, a path squiggles up the other side of the valley to **Fan y Big** but that's not our way today.

Instead, after dropping steeply down (E) to **Bwlch ar y Fan** (Wp.12 179M) we turn right (SSE) onto a substantial stony track. It has been suggested that this is the Roman road that linked the forts of **Dol y Gaer** to the south and **Y Gaer** - explored in 'Walk 39 **Carn Goch**' - to the west.

Although not absolutely straight, you'll no doubt appreciate the way it takes us directly back towards our starting point, particularly its consistent, easy downward gradient. Not appreciated so much is its flinty construction, not the most comfortable walking surface. After a heavily weight-sprung gate, we look across **Upper Neuadd Reservoir** and up to the ridge we walked this morning, with the opposite image view. However, now we can see it changing while continuing to put one foot in front of the other.

Eventually the track divides (Wp.13 212M) and we go left. The track's Roman antecedence suddenly disappears as it dives steeply down a gully to cross a stream worthy of its own name, **Nant y Gloesydd**, and we follow it only to clamber up the other side. Then it's through a metal barred gate and beside a conifer plantation to meet the road where we find our car (Wp.1 225M).

Undoubtedly the most walked route in the **Brecon Beacons**. Why? Not only is it the quickest and easiest way up the two highest mountains in South Wales, **Corn Du** and **Pen y Fan**, but the start is easy to find, being bang on the A470. Add in a decently sized car park with the rare luxury of toilets and one can't be surprised. All that said, we think the alternatives included here, **Pen y Fan from Cwm Llwch** (Route 25) and **Pen y Fan from Blaen Taf Fechan** (Route 26), are both more interesting. This route takes us directly up but returns to the **Storey Arms Centre** along a slightly less popular path.

Access by car:
From **Merthyr Tydfil**, take the A470 towards **Brecon**. Seven miles north of the roundabout with the A465 **Heads of the Valley** road and shortly after the A4059 turning to the left, we come to the sizeable car park at **Pont ar Daf** on the right. From **Brecon**, take the A470 towards **Merthyr Tydfil** and the car park is eight miles to the south, shortly after the **Storey Arms Centre**.

Starting opposite the toilets where there is a large and informative map of the area (Wp.1 0M), we go to the far end of the car park (SE) and find an obvious path on the left between conifers (E).

Passing through a kissing gate to the right of a wooden barred gat,e we go down some cobbled stones and jump between stepping stones to cross a shallow stream. An exciting start! The two metre wide stony path rises steadily up ahead of us (NE) with walkers looking like pilgrims making for a giant altar, the table topped **Corn Du**.

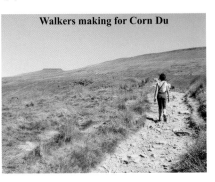

Walkers making for Corn Du

To our left, the stream which we've just crossed tumbles down over some unusual rock formations. In several places drainage channels have been cut across the path, and tessellated pavements painstakingly laid, to avoid the erosion caused by so many feet.

After forty minutes, the route divides at **Bwlch Duwynt** (Wp.2 40M) and we fork left to leave the main path and make straight for **Corn Du** (N), impatient for our first summit. Here (Wp.3 55M), as on the top of **Pen y Fan**, beware the near-vertical drop of two hundred metres on the north side. We can see the second summit to our right - only thirteen metres higher than we are - and cross to it (E) using a well worn path along the ridge. From **Pen y Fan** (Wp.4 68M) there are magnificent views in all directions. On a clear day, it's possible to see as far as **Cadair Idris** in **Snowdonia** to the north, the **Preseli Hills** to the west and **Exmoor** to the south.

Retracing our steps back along the ridge (W) to **Corn Du** (Wp.3 100M), we carefully descend on the opposite side of the table top onto the **Craig Cwm Llwch** ridge (NW). This is the only part of the route which may cause any difficulty, but if this is the case or visibility is poor, back the way we came is only sensible; easy access can easily mask the inherent dangers of walking in the mountains.

The descent after Wp.3

The stone pillar

Carrying on, we ignore a fork to the left, which is a more direct route down to the **Storey Arms Centre**, and head towards an inscribed stone pillar (Wp.5 115M).

The inscription reads:

This obelisk
marks the spot
where the body of
Tommy Jones
aged 5 was found.
He lost his way
between Cwmllwch
farm and the Login
on the night of August 4th 1900.
After an anxious search
of 29 days his remains
were discovered Sept 2nd.
Erected by voluntary subscriptions.

W. Powell Price
Mayor of Brecon 1900

The sad story retells that while staying with his grandfather at Cwm Llwch Farm, Tommy Jones disappeared and despite a search of several weeks no sign of him could be found. With a prescient reminder that tabloid journalism hasn't changed much, the 'Daily Mail' offered a reward of twenty pounds to anyone who could solve the mystery and eventually his body was found high up on the ridge, much further than it had been thought he could have wandered. The finder put the reward toward the memorial stone in his memory.

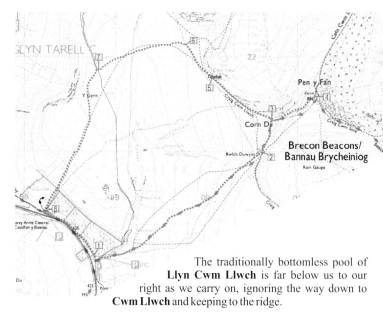

The traditionally bottomless pool of **Llyn Cwm Llwch** is far below us to our right as we carry on, ignoring the way down to **Cwm Llwch** and keeping to the ridge.

At a further divide in the path (Wp.6 125M) we take the left fork (W) which sweeps around left a total of ninety degrees going gently down before reaching a fence which bars our way (Wp.7 139M). And there are no signs! Following the fence a little to our right we find a gate to pass through; the fence looks newly erected, and our guess is that by the time of publication this 'problem' will have been sorted.

As we descend more steeply (SW) we expect to be able to see our next landmark, the **Storey Arms Centre**, but it is hidden by a plantation of conifers. Never mind, our direction can be confirmed by the path that comes down from **Fan Fawr** on the opposite side of the valley and keeping to the right hand edge of the plantation we arrive back at the road (Wp.8 163M) and the welcoming mobile burger bar in the layby on the other side. A short walk along the grass verge (SE) returns us to **Pont ar Daf** (Wp.1 169M).

This route up **Fan y Big** is easier and shorter than its sister **Llanfrynach** (Walk 29) and serves as an ideal next step after the ever popular **Pen y Fan from Pont ar Daf** (Walk 27). After crossing fields, it climbs the **Cefn Cyff** ridge between **Cwm Oergwm** and **Cwm Cynwyn** to the summit and returns down what is purported to be the Roman road over the Beacons.

3/4 4H 1M 8.1 miles/13km 550m 550m 2

Access by car:
Coming from **Brecon**, head towards **Abergavenny** on the A40 and, shortly after leaving the town, turn off the dual carriageway onto the B4558 towards **Talybont-on-Usk**. Take the first turn on the right signposted 'Llanfrynach' and the first turning on the right off that, the roads becoming narrower by the minute. At a T-junction turn right again and after ignoring a turn on the left, pass a church on the same side to park opposite a post box in a wall just before a lane leading to the Riding Centre at **Upper Cantref Farm**.

A shorter alternative
Drive up to Wp.6 **Pen-yr-heol** by taking the turning on the left after the T junction described in the directions below and walk from there up to **Fan y Big**, returning the same way.

A longer alternative
Follow Walk 29's route up to **Fan y Big** and descend using this route from Wp.9 back to Wp.1 at **Cantref Bridge**, returning to **Llanfrynach** along the road.

From our car parking spot (Wp.1 0M) we return back down the road the way we've come (E) passing the green gates of the churchyard and turn right (Wp.2 2M) down a dark, sunken, rocky and muddy lane (S). Given the chance, we're happy to leave it when we spy a footbridge over the **Afon Cynrig** to our left.

Cribyn and Pen y Fan ahead

On its other side, we go half right across a field to head towards the left of a ruined building where a stile takes us back down to rejoin the muddy lane which has forded the river without us. After a few paces to the left (Wp.3 8M) we climb the right bank up to a stile and a path that takes us alongside a right hand field edge through clover to another stile. Another field edge leads us to a gate and a road (Wp.4 13M) where we go right with **Cribyn** and **Pen y Fan** straight ahead. Then it's almost immediately left through a wooden barred gate to follow a further succession of right hand field edges that take us around to the left (SE) to a stile by a rusty barred gate and another road (Wp.5 19M).

Now its right (SSW) and after ignoring a lane to the left, we begin a steady climb, swinging left (SE) up to **Pen-yr-heol** (Wp.6 39M). Turning right in front of the barn (SW) you might pass walkers who are pulling on their boots having opted to drive to this point (our shorter alternative) before following a sunken lane up to a gate where we pass into open moorland. It's along the right hand field edge to start, then left to steeply climb up the bluff on a wide grassy path between bracken. After this serious exertion, the path climbs less steeply between clumps of marsh grass even though there is little sign of water. Our route is up the ridge all the way to our primary objective of **Fan y Big**, with the sister bluff on our left explored on Walk 29. After leaving the bracken for heather we reach the first of three cairns built to assist finding the way down in the mist (Wp.7 71M). The second is opposite a dew pond and now we see our other sister bluff to the right, reaching up to **Cribyn** with a clear stripe stretching horizontally along it half way up, the track we'll follow this afternoon.

... beautiful swirling patterns ...

After the way becomes a little steeper we come to a fork (Wp.8 92M), either path will do as the alternatives rejoin, then the going changes to bare earth between tussocky grass.

The way becomes almost flat and grassy again before our final assault on the summit. First we go left of it, enjoying beautiful swirling patterns down to our left, made by the many burgeoning watercourses at the head of **Cwm Oergwm**.

On the diving board, the route up Cribyn behind

Then turning right (N), it's just a few steps to the top with its famous diving board (Wp.9 123M).

We retrace the few steps we've just taken and go around to the right along the top of the escarpment, then down a gravel path (W) to **Bwlch ar y Fan**. Now we see **Upper Neuadd Reservoir** to our left, stopping to enjoy this view as the pieces of slate that have been used to reinforce the path that zigzags down aren't easy underfoot. Reaching the bottom, it's quite a relief to cross slabs to a stile, to the meeting of ways at the top of the pass (Wp.10 139M).

Here we just touch **Pen y Fan from Taf Fechan** (Walk 26) as it comes down towards us from **Cribyn** then follows the track to our left. We do the opposite thing, turning right (N) down the selfsame, ancient track to begin our return.

After a steep start over pieces of green slate, we swing left (NW) with a seemingly purposeless barbed wire fence to our right and rock cliff to our left. Now the way is steadily down and we swing back to the right (NNE), half way between valley bottom and ridge top with the view ahead stunning. Underfoot the surface is made up of irregularly shaped rocks so, where possible, the grass to the right of the track offers a more comfortable option. As we descend we cross a stream and, incongruously, there is gorse to our left but bracken to our right. A fence and dry stone wall on the right (Wp.11 180M) contain what appears to be a conifer plantation which turns out to be just a windbreak. Voices might be heard from above, if there are walkers on the path that comes, somewhat precipitously, directly down from **Cribyn**. After it joins us from the left we reach a wooden gate (Wp.12 194M) which marks the end of our descent.

Where the track becomes tarmacked (Wp.13 198M) we eschew this easy alternative, finding a wooden barred gate to the right that takes us down a rocky path (NE) between high hedges that obviously doubles as a watercourse after a downpour.

It swings right and widens to a track, then goes left through a rusty barred gate to become a sunken lane (Wp.14 206M) but reverts to a rocky path between hedge topped banks before meeting a road which swings in front of us from the left (Wp.15 217M). The road meanders left and right but keeps in the same general direction until coming to a T-junction (Wp.16 224M), where we turn left across the bubbling **Nant Sere**. Another road joins us from the left and we march onward (NNE) to another T-junction (Wp.17 229M) where we turn right to find our car parked on the left (Wp.1 241M). A reviving cup of tea can be obtained in the cafe at the Riding Centre.

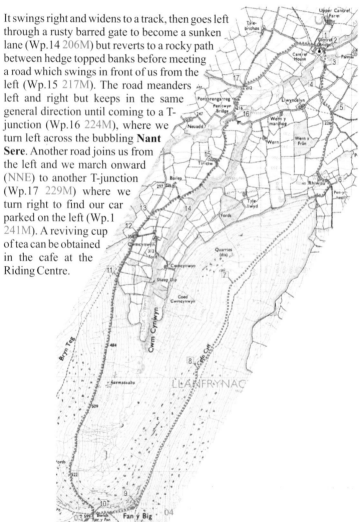

This route ascends **Fan y Big**, as does Walk 28, to its spectacular diving board summit overlooking **Cwm Cynwyn**. Each route has its unique highpoints; **Llanfrynach's** include the following of the escarpment for one hundred and eight degrees around the bowls of **Cwm Cwareli** and **Cwm Oergwm** to **Fan y Big**, and the contrasting return to the village through delightful woodland by the bubbling **Nant Menasgin**. And that's not counting the reward of **The White Swan**!

A longer alternative can be made by following this route to **Fan y Big** and descending from it via Walk 28, returning from **Cantref Bridge** to **Llanfrynach** along the lane.

Access by car:
Coming from **Brecon**, head towards **Abergavenny** on the A40 and, shortly after leaving the town, turn off the dual carriageway onto the B4558 towards **Talybont-on-Usk**. Take the first turn on the right signed 'Llanfrynach' and park in the village on the right opposite the church by public toilets.

The church at the start of the route

From our parking spot opposite the church (Wp.1 0M) we continue in the same direction (SE) and turn right into a lane signed 'Taff Trail'. After a bridge over the attractive **Nant Menasgin** we reach a junction opposite a towering horse chestnut tree (Wp.2 4M) and turn right into **Tregaer Road** (SW).

Initially the surroundings are residential, but soon we find ourselves stretching our legs on a quiet rural lane that serves the few farms in the valley. After ignoring a right fork to **Tregaer Farm** we turn left and cross a stile to the right of a wooden barred gate signed 'Rhiw Bwlch y Ddwyallt' (Wp.3 13M) which takes us onto a tarmacked track between high hedges (SE). We drop down, gently at first, but after an open metal barred gate, steeply, until we reach a concrete bridge. Then it's inevitably up again, with the series of ridges dropping down from the Beacons making their presence felt to our right.

Where the tarmac ends (Wp.4 22M), the derelict but still attractive farmhouse at **Tir-hir** is to the left while we cross a stile to the right and continue along the top of a field (SW) to another stile by a metal barred gate. Here we follow a waymark sign to the left up the side of a wood by a fence (S) and a grassy path takes us up to the top of the wood to find a stile by a metal barred gate (Wp.5 28M).

After stopping to enjoy the magnificent views back to **Llanfrynach** church, we continue between bracken in the same direction, climbing steeply until a larger path joins us from the left (Wp.6 36M). Now the going is easier, and we continue slightly upward, going left where there's a divide (Wp.7 40M) to head towards **Pen y Bryn** but then slightly right (SW) to pass it by.

There are several paths between the bracken but the main, obvious one takes us through to an area of windswept gorse bushes and then to scrubby grass. As we gain altitude the path becomes muddy, with the occasional rock strategically positioned to trip us and the few damp patches you'd expect.

Almost the whole extent of our walk is now visible, with **Llanfrynach** church far down behind us in the valley and the summit of **Fan y Big** ahead and to the right. A short clamber up to the left (SSE) takes us to the top of the ridge (Wp.8 64M) where we turn right to join a path running along it (SSW). The route is up **Gist Wen** to **Rhiw Bwlch y Ddwyallt** where a fantastic view down to the left opens up; an area explored in 'Walk 30 **Talybont Reservoir**'. After passing **Waun Rydd** on our left we reach a point where several paths meet (Wp.9 100M) and turn right (W) along **Bwlch y Ddwyallt** and the top of the escarpment. It's steeply up to start along an obvious rocky path but soon it swings left (SW) and flattens off. A cairn (Wp.10 105M) marks where we could leave the path to find the local, undistinguished highest point of 754 metres and is also the highest point of our day.

Following the escarpment south-west

All along here it's steep down to our right as we circle the bowl of **Cwm Cwareli**, swinging around to our right (W) while on the left it's flat and sandy. Where the top of the escarpment turns sharp left we have no choice but to follow it south-west onto **Craig Cwareli** to look down into the larger bowl of **Cwm Oergwm** and forward to the ridge of **Craig Oergwm**. After passing over a jumble of rocks that make progress awkward and a bald area on the left where even the most stubborn of grass can't find a purchase, we cross an area of natural pavement to reach a larger cairn (Wp.11 128M). Here we can see beyond the plateau on our left to **Pentwyn Reservoir** in the far distance. Our way is right again (W) and gently down, crossing more pavement, this time the National Park version, and on reaching the col we can see the **Neuadd Reservoirs** down to our left and the trail up to **Pen y Fan** clearly ahead.

Just after starting to ascend again (Wp.12 140M) we turn right (NNW) to thread our way between old quarry workings to climb the ridge towards **Fan y Big** with **Cwm Oergwm** now on our right.

Reaching it (Wp.13 154M), the piece of rock that sticks out like a diving board over the next valley of **Cwm Cynwyn** is as impressive as we've been led to believe.

The 'diving board' at Wp.13

To begin our descent we don't head directly down the ridge, but retrace our steps for twenty metres and then turn sharp left (NNE).

Our way ahead is clear, steadily down to start, then gently down over patches of bare volcanic earth. A patchwork of classically British fields lie ahead, with similar ridges to ours of **Bryn Teg** and **Gist Wen** left and right respectively as we pass across a carpet of heather. Where the path divides (Wp.14 177M) we choose right but either will do as the alternatives soon come together and we reach a small cairn on the right (Wp.15 194M). This is followed by two more small cairns close to the path, the second in an area where clumps of bullrushes abound; strange because the surrounding land is bone dry - I'd guess this is not always so!

The going becomes steeper as we approach the end of the bluff and we pass between straggling gorse, then luxuriant bracken. Where there's another choice of paths (Wp.16 212M) we decide on the steeper, left hand one which joins with a path that's come around the hill from the left, to arrive at a metal barred gate (Wp.17 216M). The rock-strewn sunken lane on the other side bends to the left and presents us with some difficult going until, after another gate, we arrive at **Pen-yr-heol Barn** (Wp.18 220M), now converted to holiday accommodation, where we turn left (WNW) to join a tarmacked lane signed 'Llanfrynach'.

The barley field after Wp.19

Now gently down between high hedges, we pass an attractive cottage with a slate roof before the lane swings around to the right (NNE) and becomes steeper.

After it flattens off we go through a wooden barred gate on our right (Wp.19 226M) and head diagonally left (NE) through a field of barley with a series of bluffs ahead. Before reaching the field's corner we cross a stile left of a metal barred gate and follow the next field's right hand.

Reaching a lane (Wp.20 233M) we go through a gate on the opposite side and this time follow the left hand field edge gently down to reach the boundary fence of **Tynllwyn Farm** which we follow round to find a gate in the hedge (Wp.21 238M).

'Llanfrynach' is helpfully signed again and we follow a predominantly beech hedge, cross a stile to the right of a metal barred gate and then head diagonally left towards a signpost. Here we turn right following a 'Path Legally Diverted' sign and the path becomes a track which follows a stream to the point where it joins the **Nant Menasgin** (Wp.22 246M). A signpost directs us to the left (N) through a gate and across a stream to a meadow with the sound of the river bubbling to our right.

Entering a wood through another gate (NE), we alternate between wood and river bank until another gate takes us out of it and we cross a concrete bridge over a tiny tributary of the main flow. A kissing gate to the right of a metal barred gate (Wp.23 262M) takes us out onto a lane where we turn right (E) to return to the village and find our car waiting for us along to the right (Wp.1 267M). **The White Swan** - recommended - is further on, around to the left and on the right.

A route of two contrasting halves; the first is hard work, starting below the dam of the **Talybont Reservoir**, it climbs a series of ridges to the summit of **Carn Pica** then circles around to drop back down into the **Caerfanell Valley**. The second drops gently down through the forest that runs right along the valley following the **Taff Trail**. The morning provides stunning wide views of a seemingly everlasting series of mountain ridges while the afternoon is spent wandering through cool trees with glimpses of the beautiful tract of water, which gives its name to this walk.

* but there are 3 pubs in Talybont, 1½ miles from start

Access by car:

Coming from **Brecon**, head towards **Abergavenny** on the A40 and, shortly after leaving the town, turn off the dual carriageway onto the B4558 which runs alongside the Monmouthshire and Brecon Canal to **Talybont-on-Usk**. In the village turn right following signs to 'Talybont Reservoir' to cross an unusual lifting bridge over the canal, then pass through **Aber** to reach a car park on the left, in front of a campsite managed by Welsh Water.

From the car park (Wp.1 0M), we return down the road towards **Aber** (N) between high hedges, making the most of the descent as it won't last long! At the first junction (Wp.2 3M) we turn left (WSW) into a tiny lane signed 'I'l Bryn' and immediately start climbing steadily with **Tor y Foel** dominant behind us. Where the lane goes right (Wp.3 10M) we follow a footpath straight on (SW), also signed 'I'l Bryn', which takes us through a metal barred gate between bracken.

The way is now slightly upward as we ignore a stile on our left and begin to follow a stream to our right which swings to the right (W) between an avenue of trees, the going becoming rocky underfoot. After wooden and metal barred gates in quick succession we reach a signpost (Wp.4 15M) to 'Talybont Reservoir' left and 'Twyn Du/Carn Pica' straight on; the latter is our way.

Now it's steadily up again on an attractive path through woodland, crossing the stream to its opposite bank. After a stile to the left of a metal barred gate we re-cross the stream and head away from it (SW) up the hill, the reservoir now visible below. Still climbing steadily, we come to a fork (Wp.5 25M) where we keep left and, looking back, are now high enough to see the reservoir's dam and beyond **Tor y Foel** to **Pen Cerrig-calch**.

After crossing a boggy patch we follow to the right of a fence on top of a dry stone wall. Ignoring a path left, we swing right (W) and climb steeply, the gradient easing as we near the ridge top. What's now a wide grassy path passes a cairn to our right (Wp.6 43M); its significance eludes us. We make for the peak visible ahead, now between heather in contrast to the virulent bracken which we were forced to push aside lower down. But it's a false peak and, while taking a breath, you might marvel at how much like a tree **Nant Tarthwynni** and its many tiny tributaries look when viewed from above.

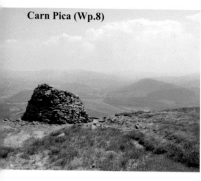

Carn Pica (Wp.8)

The next (true) peak is **Twyn Du** (Wp.7 49M) and from there it's gently down and across on the flat before attacking the escarpment ahead. The way is steep - very steep, with large earth steps aiding us here and there, and the view behind of the bluff and the valleys both sides is magnificent. We make out our premier objective, **Carn Pica** (Wp.8 87M) long before we reach it, thanks to its large beehive-looking cairn.

From our high point of the day, we ignore a path to the left which runs along the top of the escarpment and carry straight on, gently down, the land dropping steeply to our right. Curving right (NW), our way is sandy and flat with a patchwork of agriculture, so alien to our current environs, way, way down to our right. A small cairn marks a division of routes where we go left, making for the outline of **Pen y Fan** in the distance.

The ridge of **Graig Fan Las**, which we'll traverse, is ahead, but we must cross the intervening valley first. Meeting a series of muddy gullies where the land has dropped away the way becomes unclear, but after crossing a couple of them and heading downhill and to the left we meet a larger path (Wp.9 113M) where we turn right (WNW).

As soon as we drop to the valley floor we take a minor path left (Wp.10 116M), a short cut up to the main path along the ridge where we go left again (SSW) to follow its left side. We can't see to the right but there's a vertiginous drop to our left and spectacular views of the valley.

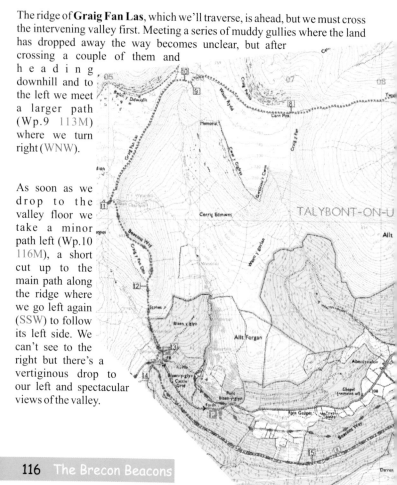

Crossing **Blaen Caerfanell** (Wp.11 145M), we watch the water disappearing down a narrow gorge before tumbling down the cliff face while we go around to the left (SSE) and slightly up onto the next ridge of **Craig y Fan Ddu**.

Again, the path follows the left side of the ridge, now with stupendous views forward, backward and downward. Also, you can just see over the ridge to our right to a further series of ridges. What a long way down we'll have to come to accomplish this afternoon's mission of ambling back through the forest. For now it's gently down a rocky path to cross to the other side of the ridge (S).

Suddenly we arrive at its end to see a road winding its way far down below us. An 'Upland Erosion Project' sign (Wp.12 162M) heralds the start of our steep descent down a staircase constructed of rocks and we head between a conifer plantation bounded by a wire fence on our left and the **Nant Bwrefwr** stream in a gully to our right.

We continue very steeply down over large rock steps, with a waterfall, partially hidden by trees, crashing away to our right, then through woodland to meet a track by a cattle grid (Wp.13 184M).

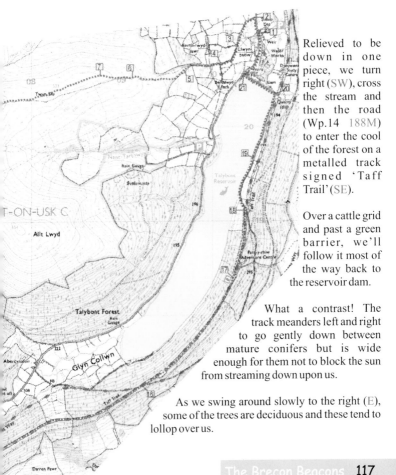

Relieved to be down in one piece, we turn right (SW), cross the stream and then the road (Wp.14 188M) to enter the cool of the forest on a metalled track signed 'Taff Trail' (SE).

Over a cattle grid and past a green barrier, we'll follow it most of the way back to the reservoir dam.

What a contrast! The track meanders left and right to go gently down between mature conifers but is wide enough for them not to block the sun from streaming down upon us.

As we swing around slowly to the right (E), some of the trees are deciduous and these tend to lollop over us.

Through gaps in the trees we see the valley down to the left and have our first view, from this direction, of **Talybont Reservoir**, which will be our constant companion, before reaching a wooden sculpture in the form of a bench (Wp.15 218M).

The smaller bench , after Wp.15

Further on is a smaller version of the same sculpture, better placed for admiring the view before coming to a crossroad of tracks (Wp.16 242M) with 'Aber Cynafon' signed left and 'Pen Rhiw-calch' right. Our way is straight across (NE) and our next landmark a footpath to **Bryn Melyn** on the right (Wp.17 261M).

Marching onward, foxgloves abound where conifers have been felled and we pass a long, low, white building on the right with its windows all barred and wonder at its possible use. After ignoring a track up to the right opposite a wide turning area, we leave the **Taff Trail** at another turn signed 'Pen Rhiw-calch' to turn right (Wp.18 271M) then immediately left to pass under a bridge.

The reservoir, after Wp.20

This boulder-strewn track overhung with trees takes us down towards the reservoir and runs parallel with it (N). Emerging from a tunnel of trees, the track widens and becomes metalled (Wp.19 280M); looking over a stile between conifers to the water's edge, we spot an idyllic camping spot.

Ahead, the reservoir's dam is glimpsed between trees and on reaching it (Wp.20 289M) we turn left to cross it, stopping to admire its entire length. At the other side (Wp.21 292M) we meet the road and turn right (NE) to follow it back past the Water Treatment Works to the car park (Wp.1 301M).

The original idea was to join the **Brecon Mountain Railway** at **Pontsticill** and travel north on it along the eastern edges of the **Pontsticill** and **Pentwyn** reservoirs to its terminus at **Dol-y-Gaer** then walk back down the other side of the reservoirs following the **Taff Trail**. But this plan was thwarted on learning that, as yet, there are no facilities for passengers to leave or join the train at **Dol-y-Gaer**. This alternative route starts at the north end of the **Pontsticill** reservoir, follows the **Taff Trail**, as planned, through the **Taff Fechan** forest to the dam at its southern end and explores a little of the wilderness area above and to the east of it before following the railway track back.

Access by car:
From the roundabout where the A470 crosses the A465 just north of **Merthyr Tydfil**, we head east on the A465 towards **Abergavenny**. Leaving at the first junction, we go right and almost immediately left across the A4054 onto a minor road that winds along the three miles to **Pontsticill**. Keeping left through the village, the **Pontsticill** reservoir appears on our right and after a further one and a half miles, we turn right and find a small car park on the left.

Walking back from the car park (Wp.1 0M S), we pass the turning and admire the beautiful view right down the reservoir towards its dam. A 'Taff Trail' signpost (Wp.2 2M) indicates the direction we should take (SW) up into the **Taf Fechan** forest and passing to the left of a green barrier, the roughly tarmacked surface of the track soon changes to blend with its environment.

We climb gently with intermittent views of the reservoir between the trees, the way sweeps away from the reservoir (W), goes down, sweeps further to the right (NW), and then gently up again ultimately becoming just a footpath. Approaching two stones standing side by side, there are dire warnings for cyclists to dismount, as the path drops steeply down to cross a narrow bridge over a gorge with a tumbling stream far below (Wp.3 17M). We guess that there must have been accidents here, but the warnings seem extreme to us. Up on the other side of the gorge and turning to the left (S), the way becomes wider again and continues to meander both from side to side and up and down as we continue through the forest.

A whistle might draw your attention to a steam train leaving **Pontsticill** station on the opposite side of the valley; we also saw a plume of smoke through a break in the trees. This attractive tourist railway runs from **Pant** station (a mile and a half south of the reservoir) to **Dol-y-Gaer** just north of **Pentwyn** reservoir, which is itself just north of **Pontsticill** reservoir. However, access to the railway is only at **Pant**, with the twenty minute stop at **Pontsticill** being for refreshments only.

A similar green barrier to the one that marked our entry signifies our exit from the forest (Wp.4 44M) and, turning right (S) into the road that we'd driven up from the village, we pass an elegant building on our left which, perhaps surprisingly, houses the water treatment works offices. An oblique turn to the

The reservoir dam at 60 minutes

left (Wp.5 50M) is our route, but if we're ready for refreshment, the two pubs in the village are just five minutes straight on; the **Red Cow** just for liquid and the **Butcher's Arms** for food as well. Returning to our route (NNE), we follow the lane down to the reservoir dam (Wp.6 60M) and slowly cross it (E) enjoying the vista of its whole two mile length.

At the other side of the dam (Wp.7 62M), we follow the lane around to the right (S) ignoring the one to the left which would seem the obvious direction to go. Ten minutes down the hill we reach a footpath that goes up to our left (Wp.8 72M), opposite the turn into the **Pontsticill Water Treatment Works**. The signpost for the footpath reads 'Talybont', an objective a tad ambitious for today! A steady pace is advised up here (NE), partly because of the steep gradient, but mostly because the stunning views of the reservoir, with the chain of **Corn Du**, **Pen y Fan**, **Cribyn** and **Fan y Big** providing a fantastic backdrop, deserve frequent stops.

The start is on a grassy path (the drystone wall on the left rebuilt by a volunteer group) and we cross a track before passing under a railway bridge which, strangely, has a metal barred gate right in the middle of it. The way is now stony with the railway down to our left as we approach two metal gates. Our route is through the smaller one to the right, and we continue climbing, now on a grassy path again, between bracken. Presented with a choice of grassy paths, we take the right fork up to a high, rusty gate, entangled with barbed wire, as if the farmer believes he has a Houdini amongst his sheep (Wp.9 98M).

This takes us through into an area of open moorland, criss-crossed with sheep tracks. The route is not always entirely clear but this is not normally a problem as there are obvious landmarks. But if visibility is poor we wouldn't advise continuing, because there is a potentially dangerous drop into an old quarry working and many *shake holes*, a geographical feature of the **Brecon Beacons** where the underlying limestone has collapsed.

... the reservoir, our constant companion

Taking the path to our left (N), we walk parallel to a drystone wall looking over it down to the reservoir, our constant companion. To our right, a little further up the hill but running almost parallel to us, is a track that has become churned up by weekend off road bikers, but they are too far away to bother us.

Passing close to the edge of the old quarry workings mentioned (Wp.10 116M) we have yet another great photographic opportunity with the reservoir beyond. Bearing slightly to our right from here (NE), we make for the right hand side of a conifer plantation on the other side of a small, river valley.

Down in the valley we spot a crude, collapsed vehicle bridge that crosses the river, but just to its left is a railway sleeper (Wp.11 130M) which has been placed judiciously for us to balance across. On the other side, we follow a more distinct track than we've become accustomed to, and just when it seems this must be the wrong way because we're going away from the plantation, we see a small path on our left (Wp.12 134M) which takes us back along the top of it (W). Passing the end of the plantation, the way becomes indistinct again but continuing in the same direction, we find a footpath (Wp.13 156M) into another plantation, this time of newly planted trees.

The way goes steeply down, and ignoring a footpath that goes off to our right through mature trees, we continue down between newly planted trees on our left and mature ones on our right. We know that we must find a way of crossing the railway and suddenly, we see down to our left a bridge with what looks like a hole in the ground in front of it. This is it (Wp.14 162M), and we are amazed to emerge onto a gravel track.

The hole in the ground at Wp.14

Turning right (N), we crunch along the gravel beside the railway, passing a sailing club on our left which we'd noticed from between the trees when on the other side of the reservoir. Where the track crosses the railway on a level crossing (Wp.15 166M) we stay on the same side, now on a path alongside the line.Eventually path and track diverge, and we walk down to the water and along it until we reach a lane (Wp.16 182M) where we turn left (W) to cross between the **Pentwyn** and **Pontsticill** reservoirs, and so back to the car park (Wp.1 191M).

This route, full of variety, takes us up the **Taf Fawr** valley mainly following the route of the **Taff Trail**. It passes the **Llwyn on**, **Cantref** and **Beacon** reservoirs on the opposite side of the valley from the main **Merthyr Tydfil** to **Brecon** road. Our objective is the **Storey Arms Centre** from where we catch a bus back to our start point. (2 hourly service; the 15.15 bus will probably be most useful.) The incline is rarely more than gentle, so you'll be surprised at how much height we gained by the time you're returning on the downward sweeping bus journey. Views over the three reservoirs and ahead to the peaks of **Fan Fawr** (Route 24) and **Pen y Fan** (Routes 25, 26 and 27) are superb.

Access by car, and return to the car by bus:
From **Merthyr Tydfil**, we take the A470 towards **Brecon**. Two miles north of the roundabout with the A465 Heads of the Valley road, following prominent signs to a camp site, there's a lane to the left signed **Cwm Cadlan**; park just past this in a layby opposite an attractive wooden bus shelter. On return, ask the bus driver for the **Llwyn on Village** stop.

Short Alternative
A delightful shorter alternative is to simply circle the **Llwyn on** reservoir.
(1 walker, 2 hours)

Walking back from the layby (Wp.1 0M), we take the narrow lane now to our right (NW) signed **Cwm Cadlan**. The magnificent vista across **Llwyn on** reservoir opens up ahead (Wp.2 4M) as we follow the lane across the dam (SW) with its gothic-looking turrets. At the other side (Wp.3 9M), the lane swings right to join the **Taff Trail** and follows the edge of the reservoir (NW).

A well planned car park with picnic benches and map of the reservoir showing points of interest (Wp.4 11M) appears to our right but we continue, an attractive hedge on our right. We find several further picnic sites along here, some of which have paths leading down to the edge of the reservoir; good examples of non-intrusive tourist development by the Brecon Beacons National Park management. Passing a lane off to **Cwm Cadlan** (Wp.5 22M N) we continue

beside the reservoir until the sound of a waterfall and a stile to our right beckon (Wp.6 35M). Six log steps down and a few paces to our left take us to the source of the noise. Continuing on the lane again, another lane comes down from the left signed **Garwnant Forest Centre**. Eventually this will be our way, but now we travel on (NE) to reach a green girder bridge (Wp.7 48M) over the tumbling **Taf Fawr**.

On the far side of the bridge and to the right is a shaded picnic site, and in the far left corner of this is a stile that leads onto a path to take us back to our starting point to form the Short Alternative Walk.

Returning across the bridge, we take the right fork up (SW) to the **Garwnant Forest Centre** (Wp.8 55M) a series of log cabins which house not only a café and shop, but also a classroom. There's also an adventure playground, cycle hire and a fascinating map of the area carved from wood.

The wooden map

Not too obviously, our route is to the right of the buildings and to the far side of the car park where a wooden 'Taff Trail' signpost (N) guides us to a gravel track through coniferous woods which swings right while we go straight on (Wp.9 65M), now following the sign of a white footprint on a green background, and passing to the right of a green barrier with three diagonal white stripes. The way is now a muddy track which leads us by a forbidding stone building, clearly not occupied but with green corrugated iron topped by circles of barbed wire - wonder what its use was? In stark contrast, the view to our right across the valley is stunning.

Continuing along what has become a well defined woodland path, we cross two streams, the second of them on stepping stones, to reach a crossroad of footpaths with a signpost; to the left is signed 'A4059', to the right, 'Pont Llysiog' but no destination is given for our route straight ahead! However, we continue confidently in the same direction even though the going is sometimes muddy, passing a ruined building on the right until the path swings left (Wp.10 75M W). A short climb follows, the first of only two significant gradients in our route. The trees to the right have been felled, beyond a gully from which a tinkle of water emanates. Levelling off, we reach a gravel firebreak (Wp.11 80M) and turn right (N), joining the white footprint on green background sign again.

Ascending gently, to our right are magnificent views of the next reservoir up the valley, the **Cantref**, and across to the main road. Ahead is the surreal view of vehicles moving across the skyline; the A4059 which we cross later. After an open space and a track diagonally off to the left, the firebreak deteriorates to become two paths with waist-high grass between them; it's clear that no vehicle has been along here for some time. Reaching the edge of the woodland area, we cross a stile (Wp.12 118M) into a boggy field, still enjoying glorious views across the valley and of our return bus route. A muddy path takes us across many streams that tumble down into the valley, a couple of them being substantial enough to require wooden footbridges.

Over a stile back into woodland (Wp.13 134M) we encounter a signpost with the 'Taff Trail' symbol, only in evidence here and there. This is a mystical woodland path to savour, which leads us to another wooden bridge, this time with handrails both sides, a waterfall tumbling down to our left. Coming to a padlocked metal barred gate, we cross a stile (Wp.14 145M) to reach the main road.

Taff Trail sign

To our right, the road crosses the river, water tumbling over a weir beneath it, but we go across it and slightly along to the right into a car parking area opposite, and then between some gateposts up a track into a wood. Ignoring two further tracks to our right (the first of which gives access to a noisy generator in a dirty white building), we climb up through a wood. This is the second serious incline, but once again, it's over quite soon. Through a gap in the trees to our left (Wp.15 157M), we see a path to the edge of the wood and a stile out of it at a wooden signpost with the 'Taff Trail' symbol on it.

First, the path runs to the right (N) along the edge of the wood but then meanders away from it to reach an unlikely precipitous place, half way up a sizeable gully gouged out by the tiny **Nant Pennig**. We cross it (Wp.16 165M), making use of some really good stepping stones. Further on the path becomes indistinct and boggy; unfortunately a 'feature' of walking in the Brecon Beacons is that where the going becomes boggy, previous walkers have found their own way round it, obscuring the 'official' way and making it difficult to find. Here, as elsewhere, if we carry on in the same direction (N) the path reappears, and before long we see our goal ahead and down on our right, the **Storey Arms Centre** with its distinctive red telephone box. Reaching a grass covered earthwork (Wp.17 191M) we follow it down to the right and to the road (Wp.18 195M). There's a burger bar in the layby for modest refreshments while waiting for the bus to take us back to our starting point. Flag it down by the telephone box on the other side.

33 WATERFALLS

This is the classic waterfall walk in the **Brecon Beacons** where the rivers **Mellte**, **Hepste**, **Nedd** and **Pyrddin** all plunge over a series of waterfalls, the best examples in Wales. However, instead of the normal start at **Pontneddfechan**, it begins half way around near the **Clun Gwyn** waterfalls enabling a lunchtime pub stop. It's best to choose a day when it's rained the night before as the falls will be at their best, in full flow. Also be aware that this walk is more tiring than the distance would indicate due to the many tricky, rocky stretches; if in any doubt choose **Sgwd yr Eira** (Walk 34) instead.

Access by car:
From the roundabout where the A470 crosses the A465 just north of **Merthyr Tydfil**, head west on the A465 towards **Neath** and leave the dual carriageway for the A4109 signposted 'Dyffryn'. At traffic lights, turn right then fork left following signs for 'Pontneddfechan' and look out for **The Angel** on the left, our lunchtime watering hole. Take a left signed 'Ystradfellte', finding our car park after three miles, the gravel covered area on the right, just before a cattle grid, by a sign for 'Clun Gwyn Farm and Bunkhouse'.

> **Easier Alternative**
> A much easier, but still really delightful, alternative is to start from 'The Angel' at **Pontneddfechan** (Wp.15) and walk up to **Sgwd Gwladys** (Wp.19), returning the same way.

From the car park (Wp.1 0M) we walk down a track (ENE) towards **Clun Gwyn**. After crossing a stream, we go through a kissing gate to the right of a metal barred gate and pass a Brecon Beacons information board before coming to a fork where we go right, following the advised route to the waterfalls. After another kissing gate it's gently down, now on a wide woodland path, ignoring a path on our right (Wp.2 7M) to 'Sgwd Isaf Clun Gwyn', before we begin to hear the roar of rushing water. As it gets louder we glimpse the falls, a tumble of chaotic whiteness between the trees. A fence between us and it ensures our patience a little longer before getting close so we hurry along a path strewn with roots and rocks (N) to cross a wooden footbridge (Wp.3 13M). There's a stile straight in front of us but we turn right (S) to follow the bank of the **Afon Mellte** along a treacherously rocky path.

Where there's a choice, we go to the left up into woods rather than staying close to the river but can still hear it and before long emerge to look down on **Sgwd Uchaf Clun Gwyn**, the falls we'd earlier seen from the other side of the river. Continuing, we reach conifers on our left, a wooden barrier to our right and then a path to the left signed to **Gwaun Hepste** and **Sgwd yr Eira** (Wp.4 19M). Although **Sgwd yr Eira** is most certainly on our agenda today, we go right, so steeply down we need to hang onto the wooden barriers, to reach **Sgwd Isaf Clun Gwyn**. Then we follow the river, splashing through a couple of streams until our path goes around to the left and the river has dropped so far down that we're high above it again, squeezing along the foot of a cliff. After it swings back to the right again (W), the sound of the water gets louder again. but at a split in the path (Wp.5 31M), we scramble up to the left (SSE) rather than following the river steeply down right. The way is rocky and a little overgrown until it runs along the top of the steepest part of the cliff, then it's up to the left (NE) to meet a larger path where we turn right (Wp.6 37M SSE). To the left are conifers and, after ignoring a path on our right, we go round them to the left (ENE) to pass between the **Mellte** and the **Hepste** valleys by an admirably positioned bench. After hearing the sound of **Sgwd yr Eira** ahead, and just after a second bench, we turn right (Wp.7 44M), following the signs to it down steps (S) past a board with dire warnings of the dangers ahead which only serve to heighten the anticipation.

... the waterfall crashes down ...

The warnings are unusually realistic as the steps that take us zigzagging down the steep cliff are uneven, muddy and slippery but, reaching the bottom (Wp.8 53M), the effort is worth it as the water rushes by our feet and the waterfall crashes down to our left. From here, it's difficult to believe that we'll be walking behind it! We edge our way extremely carefully towards it on the narrow, wet and rocky way.

Passing behind the waterfall is an incredible experience not to be missed. There's enough space, but the quantity and intensity of spray means that keeping dry is not an option; you could don waterproofs, but it would spoil the experience. Back up the other side (SW) it's rocky and muddy again, twisting and turning with steps and a rail to hang onto half way up. At the top we reach an open, grassy space with an enormous rock (Wp.9 64M) and turn right.

Now the going is completely different, first up and down through woodland with bracken our constant companion, then grassy to the left with rocks underfoot before we swing right at a conifer wood, descending then swinging left again. After crossing a stream it's rocky before we cross another stream on a slatted bridge (Wp.10 81M) where glorious views of the valley ahead open up.

A rusty gate (Wp.11 93M) leads us over a boggy patch and gently down (WSW) to a smaller path on our right (Wp.12 99M) where the clamouring **Afon Mellte**, its force now doubled by its confluence with the **Hepste**, makes its presence known again. A large path on our left signed 'Penderyn' joins us (Wp.13 103M), and a steep chasm containing the much smaller **Afon Sychryd** becomes apparent. Our wide grassy path begins dropping steeply, becoming increasingly rocky until we reach a car park, half enclosed by grey cliffs, at **Craig y Dinas** (Wp.14 111M), from where we turn right to cross a bridge over the river, then left to follow its opposite bank.

Suddenly, we're jolted back into civilization as we pass down the road between an ugly, breeze-block bus shelter and **Pontneddfechan's** modern semi-detached houses. After the junction with the road to **Ystradfellte** we took earlier, **The Craig y Dinas Hotel** on the left and **The Old White Horse** down a side street on the right are lunch alternatives to **The Angel** (Wp.15 129M).

Facing the pub again, we go behind it and to its right to pass to the left of a

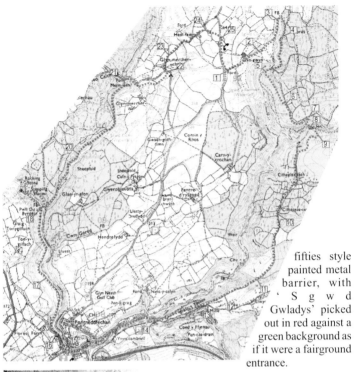

fifties style painted metal barrier, with ' S g w d Gwladys' picked out in red against a green background as if it were a fairground entrance.

... classically beautiful waterfall ...

Our extremely well-defined path runs alongside **Afon Nedd** (N) through deciduous woodland; truly delightful. After a gap between a metal barred gate and a stile (Wp.16 136M), we pass a ruined building on our left almost hidden by vigorous plant life before reaching a gate (Wp.17 144M). Picnic benches on the left precede some steps up, but the going's still very easy, and we reach a footbridge (Wp.18 155M). Here we take an optional detour up the **Afon Pyrddin** to **Sgwd Gwladys**, a well known beauty spot, by turning left before crossing the footbridge (WNW) and following the path to the classically beautiful waterfall.

Reaching it, we scramble down to a grey pebble beech and cross to the other side of the river on stepping stones (Wp.19 166M).

Returning to the footbridge (Wp.18 171M), we follow the signpost to 'Pont Melin Fach' (NE) continuing beside the **Afon Nedd** as it crashes and tumbles its way down the valley. The water runs in a chasm before we cross a footbridge over one of the river's many tributaries (Wp.20 188M), the water swirls around and down beside a giant rock which attempts to bar its progress.

The magnificent Sgwd Ddwli

Ahead is the magnificent **Sgwd Ddwli** and we begin a steady climb to get above it. Then it's across another footbridge and past more smaller waterfalls before reaching the car park at **Pont Melin Fach** (Wp.21 215M) with an attractive spacious, grassy picnic area contained by a sweep in the river.

Turning right on the road (E), we cross a bridge and start steadily climbing with a stream beside us. At a track leading to **Glyn-mercher-uchaf Farm** (Wp.22 224M), we turn left (N), passing the farm on the left via a metal barred gate, as the stile beside it is surrounded by stinging nettles.

Where there's a gap in the hedges enclosing the track (Wp.23 228M), we go diagonally right, following the right hand field edge (NE) towards woods; for the first time, our path isn't obvious. But beyond the corner of the field we cross a sunken lane to a waymarked stile which takes us into a wood. Another stile to the right of a metal barred gate leads to another sunken lane that swings right and left before going through a metal barred gate to pass **Heol-fawr Farm** on the right, where the track becomes tarmacked. Where it swings left (Wp.24 235M) we turn right (ESE) and go over a stile to the left of a metal barred gate, pass to the left of two caravans and cross a stile to the left of another metal barred gate. We're in a pleasant meadow, heading for a stile on its opposite side and slightly to the right to emerge on a road opposite a chapel (Wp.25 239M). Turning right (S), we pass an isolated petrol station which, fortunately for us, sells ice creams before returning to our start point (Wp.1 244M).

If you love waterfalls and know that 'sgwd' is Welsh for 'waterfall' then you'll recognize that this one is for you! Where the sandstone that forms the **Brecon Beacons** changes to limestone, this route runs beside **Afon Mellte** to **Sgwd Clun-gwyn**, **Sgwd Isaf Clun-gwyn** and **Sgwd y Pannwr**, then to **Afon Hepste** and **Sgwd yr Eira** before returning through the woods. Each waterfall has its own character, but **Sgwd yr Eira** will undoubtedly be the highlight as you can walk right behind it! As if that isn't enough, there's the chance to visit **Porth yr Ogof**, the largest cave entrance in Wales.

2   2H 40M   4.5 miles/7.2km   100m / 100m   0*

* none on route, but pub in **Ystradfellte**

Access by car:
From the roundabout where the A470 crosses the A465 just north of **Merthyr Tydfil**, head west on the A465 towards **Neath**. At the second roundabout, turn right onto the A4059 towards **Brecon** and one mile after the village of **Penderyn** fork left onto a minor road towards **Ystradfellte**. Our objective is the car park at **Porth yr Ogof**, which is reached by taking the left fork each of the three times we're given a choice. It's one of the few National Park car parks where we have to pay, but there are decent toilets! During summer weekends it may be full, when a warden will direct you to the alternative at **Gwaen Hepste**; a waymarked path brings you back to the start.

Before embarking on the walk proper it seems a pity not to take a look at the impressive **Porth yr Ogof** cave entrance as we're almost on top of it. We find it by walking to the far end of the car park, over a stile and down steps into a limestone gorge. Here, **Afon Mellte** plunges underground to appear again 300 metres down the valley. Back at the car park again (Wp.1 0M), we cross the road slightly to our left to find a woodland footpath (SSW). Almost immediately the ways divide (Wp.2 2M) and ignoring a footpath going forward, we follow the signpost to 'Blue Pool and Waterfall'.

We go through a kissing gate to the right of a metalled barred gate, and along a well defined path, skirting woodland. As the route disappears into the woods proper we step deftly between are rocks in the path, our way looking like a dried up stream bed. Some of the larger rocks have been eroded so that they remind us of Henry Moore sculptures, and after squeezing between two of them, we cross a stream and notice **Afon Mellte**, bubbling to our right, which has reappeared after its underground journey from the cave entrance. Skirting the woods again, we pass an old-fashioned meadow which looks like a wonderful picnic spot but, unfortunately, a barbed wire fence is between us and it; you can't have everything! As we begin to climb, tree roots stretch across in front of us where earth has been washed away, and we go through another kissing gate where some rocks, although smooth, could easily turn an ankle.

... a close view of Sgwd y Pannwr ...

The river's now below; after another kissing gate and field, this time left to set-aside, we drop down to a meeting of the ways (Wp.3 31M). Left is a stile, and right is a footbridge across the river where Walk 33 (a longer waterfall walk) joins us from **Pontneddfechan**, but we go straight on (SSE), our way now a woodland path beside the river, exposed roots still hoping to trip us. Climbing above the river again, we stop to admire the view down on **Sgwd Clun-gwyn** (Wp.4 35M) and again down on **Sgwd Isaf Clun-gwyn** (Wp.5 49M) then, at a post with a green band painted on top (Wp.6 59M), we turn obliquely right back on ourselves (W) to follow posts with red bands down through lush woods for a close view of **Sgwd y Pannwr** and a paddle (Wp.7 71M).

Returning to the turnoff (Wp.6 87M) we continue on the same path (SE), climbing again and passing through a hole in a drystone wall to a conifer plantation where a rock way appears to have been laid. Circling left around the edge of another plantation (E), **Afon Hepste** audible ahead and far below.

Descending steeply, we reach a bench with views right across the valley; time for a welcome rest. Crossing a stile to our right (Wp.8 97M), we go down steep steps which twist and turn to the gorge bottom to clamber over rocks and reach our objective, **Sgwd yr Eira** (Wp.9 101M), revelling in standing behind the curtain of water without getting wet - yet it's difficult to believe that sheep used to be driven across the valley by this route.

Sgwd yr Eira

Walk 33 continues up the other side of the valley, but we climb back to the stile (Wp.8 110M) and turn right along our original path before turning left (Wp.10 112M) into the claustrophobic darkness of a conifer wood (N). Ascending steadily, using neatly constructed steps in places, we reach a track (Wp.11 116M) and turn right (ENE) onto what becomes a substantial firebreak. A wooden signpost (Wp.12 129M) indicates 'Gwaen Hepste' straight on and 'A4059' to the right, but we dive off left onto a small path between the woods (NW). Crossing a track (Wp.13 140M), the path becomes narrower still and we battle through the odd combination of brambles and bullrushes until we're surprised to meet a signpost (Wp.14 149M) for 'Gwaen Hepste' right and 'Porth yr Ogof' left; cannily, we go left, down to the right of a plantation and to a wooden stile (Wp.15 154M). Along the track to our right we find our car park (Wp.1 160M). In the summer, there may even be an ice cream van.

35 LLYN Y FAN FAWR

This is the only route that goes up into the wildness and unique raw beauty of **The Black Mountain** area which, though more walked in recent years, is still much less walked than the other areas and should not be missed. The route passes by **Allt Fach** to attain the top of the **Fan Hir** escarpment, then drops down past **Llyn y Fan Fawr** to follow the bank of **Nant y Llyn** by numerous, glorious waterfalls to cross **Afon Tawe** and return down a quiet road to complete the circle.

Access by car: From the roundabout where the A470 crosses the A465 just north of **Merthyr Tydfil**, head west on the A465 towards **Neath** and leave the dual carriageway for the A4109 signposted 'Dyffryn'. Go straight over the traffic lights, then after losing the A4109 to the left, you'll be on the A4221, heading towards **Abercraf**. Turn right onto the A4067 and after **Glyntawe** park on the left opposite **The Tafarn-y-Garreg** public house, in its car park.

From the car park (Wp.1 0M), we take a path to its left (NW) and go through a metal barred gate to cross a wooden bridge that spans the **Afon Tawe**. Turning right (NE), we follow the attractive river bank guided by a 'Permitted Access to Mountain' sign accompanied by a cacophony of cocks crowing, ducks quacking and sheep baaing, emanating from the field beside us.

A metal barred gate on our left (Wp.2 6M) leads us up a track (WNW) between fences away from the river with **Allt Fach** towering in front of us. The path takes us right through a rusty gate then to the right (N) between a sheep pen on the left and a fence on the right to pass **Ty Hendrey Farm**.

We follow this fence around to the left to a stile that takes us into open moorland and though the way's not obvious, there's an encouraging 'Beacons Way' sign. Heading half left and very steeply towards the highest point visible

(WNW), we pass to the right of an ancient settlement. After an area of abundant marsh grass the path becomes obvious. Stopping to survey the valley, you might recognize **Craig-y-Nos Castle** and **Cribarth** above it, explored in Walk 36, 'Hendryd Falls'.

After the gradient eases the main path goes to the summit of **Allt Fach** dead ahead while we fork right (Wp.3 39M N) along a smaller path from which the main road in the valley can be seen snaking up to the pass and thence to **Sennybridge**.

As we swing around the hill (NW) we see the awesome **Fan Hir** escarpment ahead which we'll be walking along the top of and remark that in reasonable weather one cannot imagine losing one's way. After crossing a stream in a gully the path swings right (NNW) and climbs to a point where the escarpment drops steeply away to our right. The distinctive outlines of **Pen y Fan** and **Corn Du** rise slightly above the lesser peaks in front of them; also intermittently visible on the left is the jumble of summits over five hundred metres, together described as the **Carmarthen Fans**.

.. horizontal sheets of rock ... (Wp.4)

Rock outcrops on our left are a geologist's delight, compressed from different rocks of varying colours (Wp.4 82M), and horizontal sheets of rock stick out from the top of the steep cliff, similar to the 'diving board' at the top of **Fan y Big** on Walk 28.

Ahead, we get our first glimpse of **Llyn y Fan Fawr** then, now walking easily on the flat, see **Usk Reservoir** in the distance before starting gently down and swinging around to the left (NW), the steep escarpment still to our right. With **Llyn y Fan Fawr** just below us, we begin to drop down to a *col* with the way up the other side very well defined. But this isn't for us, as at the lowest point we turn sharp right (Wp.5 122M E), descending the escarpment on what is locally known as **The Staircase**, to the right hand side of the lake. It's very steep and rocky at first but easier as we approach the water, which laps contentedly to itself.

Soon after leaving the lake behind (Wp.6 143M) we fork right (ESE) beside the **Nant y Llyn** which takes water down from the lake to **Afon Tawe** in the valley. Where it spreads across a wide boggy area, the well trodden path skirts to the left; though the paths here are well walked, surprisingly few are marked on OS maps. We cross the stream (Wp.7 157M) and have a clear view of **Pen y Fan** and **Corn Du** again before re-crossing it and continuing gently down. Our companion now runs in a little gully to our right and begins to drop over a series of small waterfalls that will continue all the way until it joins **Afon Tawe**.

There's one with ferns on one side and heather on the other and drops into a placid pool to make a classic picture; a more idyllic picnic spot would be

An idyllic picnic spot (Wp.8)

difficult to conjure (Wp.8 167M). Continuing after our lunch a rapidly increasing body of water now flows in a deep gorge between vibrant heather and gorse with the berries from an occasional rowan tree making a stunning colour combination.

The waterfalls, some still little some now larger, come thick and fast as our way becomes steeper. A path, not much more than a sheep track, crosses us then, followed soon after by another (Wp.9 180M). This time we are tempted right (S) and drop down in order to cross the **Nant y Llyn**, then continue along the contour.

The crossing place

After crossing another stream in a gully, the man made path becomes less defined as we continue along the contour a little further before swinging left (SE) to drop straight down to the river where we turn right (Wp.10 200M S),on a path that runs along its bank, looking for a crossing place (see photo on the next page). There's a choice between a crude rock dam and stepping stones just below it; we select the former then follow a path up the left hand side of the river. Before reaching a conifer plantation (Wp.11 211M) we follow tractor tracks across a field to our left (E) to reach a quiet road that runs down the valley, parallel to the river (Wp.12 214M).

We go right (S), and after crossing a cattle grid, pass between high hedges rich with honeysuckle, blackberries and a host of other greenery. Slowly we are reintroduced to civilization as we pass outlying farms, taking in a last view of **Cribarth** before meeting the main road (Wp13 244M) where we turn right (SW) into the whoosh of traffic - but thankfully, the pub car park is only two minutes away (Wp.1 246M). **The Tafarn-y-Garreg** inn is not only open all day, but serves a mean cream tea in the afternoon; just what the doctor ordered after our exertions of the day.

South Wales' highest waterfall is the number one attraction of this walk which we'll save 'til last; and it's not the only attraction by any means as we pass through **Craig-y-nos Country Park** with its 19th century castle, climb to the summit of **Cribarth** and return along a beautiful gorge to **Henrhyd Falls** themselves and a chance to picnic behind them! Other alternatives for lunch are at **Craig-y-nos**, one third of the way around the route, and in **Abercraf**, two thirds around. So let's get to it!

Access by car:
From the roundabout where the A470 crosses the A465 just north of **Merthyr Tydfil**, head west on the A465 towards **Neath** and leave the dual carriageway for the A4109 signed 'Dyffryn'. Straight over the traffic lights, then you'll lose the A4109 to the left and find yourself on the A4221 heading towards **Abercraf**. After taking the next turning right signed 'Coelbren', go right at the first T-junction, through the village, and left at the second to find an attractive dry stone walled car park on your left. These three turnings all have signs for 'Henrhyd Falls', so small that you'll need 20 20 vision to spot them!

From the car park (Wp.1 0M) we continue along the road (NW), with the **Carmarthen Fans** directly ahead, and just after a prominent mobile phone mast (Wp.2 7M), turn right to cross a stile. No path is immediately clear across the field but continuing slightly left of our previous direction, we see duckboards that cover a boggy patch either side of a bridge ahead. After these, the path is obvious. We go over a stile, cross more duckboards and go up the next field to arrive at a metal barred gate; however, we don't go through it but turn right to follow the fence until a waymark directs us left and down by a fence atop a bank. Funnelled between this bank and a stream on our right, we reach a metal barred gate which we pass on our left to cross a stile and reach a road (Wp.3 22M). Turning right (N) we continue downhill between woods, passing a white chapel on our right and crossing a bridge before swinging left towards the sound of rushing water. This is the bridge at **Pen-y-cae** which crosses the **Afon Tawe** but just before it we turn right up a residential 'no through' road (Wp.4 35M). A gap between metal barred gates at the road's end leads to our muddy, tree-lined path. A tarmacked lane joins us from the left and we join a wide road (Wp.5 48M) which immediately narrows. **Cribarth** is now prominent on our left; we anticipate its conquest later today.

Just after a sign to an Outdoor Adventure Centre and a bungalow on our right, we fork left down a smaller lane (Wp.6 55M NNW) to **Rhongyr-uchaf House** (Wp.7 59M). Passing it on our right via a metal barred gate, we keep left of the attractive stone wall marking its boundary and soon hear the river away to our left; we turn left (SW) through an ancient wooden gate (Wp.8 69M) to find it along a rocky path which takes us down to giant stepping stones. Disappointingly, our route isn't across them; we turn left instead to enter **Craig-y-nos Country Park** and pass along a wide path between statuesque conifers and by a spacious games and picnic area. After turning right over a bridge, we go right then left in quick succession before passing a useful map to reach the car park and our way out to the main road (Wp.9 84M).

Now it's left (SSE), passing the Teutonic looking castle (and bar), **The Coach House** and a lay-by before turning right, following a sign to 'Open Hill', via either kissing gate or stile (Wp.10 90M). The wide grassy path takes us gently up, lulling us into a false sense of security; in 100 metres a sign directs us right onto a narrow, still grassy path that climbs steadily to look down upon the castle. Following white topped posts that mark our way, we reach a fence, panting, only to climb more steeply up beside it. Given a choice we fork left (Wp.11 111M SE), still following white topped posts; this way is only slightly up yet has a fantastic view not only down the chimneys of the castle, but all the way along the valley.

Looking down on the castle

After this brief respite we reach a dry stone wall and turn right to follow it (W), steadily climbing again to a ladder stile (Wp.12 120M); its top makes an excellent place to stop before continuing up along the other side of the wall, then swinging around to the left a little (SW), first following the top of the escarpment, then going right of a limestone crag. Gently uphill now, we go through the remains of much quarrying into a natural amphitheatre, then beyond it to follow a wall which becomes a fence, until we see the trig point which marks the summit of **Cribarth** ahead and up to our right. We leave the main path (Wp.13 141M) and climb steeply to it (Wp.14 144M).

It's even steeper down the other side to our path which continues by the fence until it turns left (Wp.15 156M). There's the temptation to carry straight on by the green of a disused tramroad that runs along the side of the hill ahead, but our less obvious way is to follow the fence left, crossing it on a stile just fifty metres along from the corner. Continuing gently down, we're walking through typical moorland and become surrounded by bracken as we lose height. A stile signposted 'Abercrave' (Wp.16 165M) takes us out of moorland and onto a path, clearly one of the original quarry inclines. Now it's steadily down, slaloming between voracious stinging nettles until we reach a stile where conditions improve and we enter luscious woodland. After a further series of stiles, a gravel track joins us from the left (Wp.17 172M) but where it swings to the left we carry on down the incline on a path again. Eventually, we enter residential **Abercraf** and pass between school and fire station before reaching a larger road (Wp.18 181M) where we turn left (ENE). As mentioned in this book's introduction, many places have both Welsh and English names and where this is the case we defer to that on the Ordnance Survey map but sometimes, as here, we find many references to the alternative name. Ten minutes along the road we find the hospitable **Copper Beech** and **Abercrave** inns accompanying each other on the left (Wp.19 191M) happily demonstrating the adage that competition improves the breed.

We turn right down **Station Road** which swings right then left before crossing the **Afon Tawe** (SSE). On the near side of the first house after the bridge (Wp.20 196M) we go left through a utilitarian kissing gate (SE) and after another kissing gate, cross a field on a tarmacked path and under a main road.

Now it's through yet another kissing gate before making for a signpost where we go left alongside the river, then right and slightly uphill into woodland. A stile takes us into a meadow (Wp.21 205M).

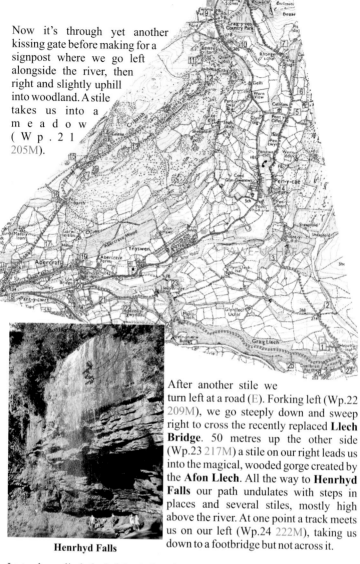

After another stile we turn left at a road (E). Forking left (Wp.22 209M), we go steeply down and sweep right to cross the recently replaced **Llech Bridge**. 50 metres up the other side (Wp.23 217M) a stile on our right leads us into the magical, wooded gorge created by the **Afon Llech**. All the way to **Henrhyd Falls** our path undulates with steps in places and several stiles, mostly high above the river. At one point a track meets us on our left (Wp.24 222M), taking us down to a footbridge but not across it.

Henrhyd Falls

Instead we climb the left bank, keeping to this side until just before the falls. After a National Trust 'Sgwd Henrhyd' sign (Wp.25 261M) we cross a footbridge and stop to gawp at a small but stunning waterfall where a tributary of the **Llech** drops over a sheer piece of rock. Then it's right down to the edge of the water and a waterfall - but this is chicken feed compared with what's to come! A gravel path on the left (Wp.26 266M) will lead us back to the car park, but first it's forward and across the gorge on a substantial wooden bridge to reach the falls themselves. After edging along a narrow ledge half way up the cliff, we reach a substantial area behind the fall which is completely dry (Wp.27 277M) and marvel at the wonderful rainbow that is created when the sun's rays meet the falling water. Reluctantly, we retrace our footsteps over the bridge back to where the paths divide (Wp.26 290M), this time going right (ENE) up through a gate into our starting car park (Wp.1 297M).

Variety, it is said, is the spice of life; and this walk offers a wide variety of ingredients. A Roman road runs from the forest car park start to our lunchtime stop at **The Cross Inn**. Our morning takes us up north of it, passing through gentle wooded valleys reminiscent of the Sussex Downs while after lunch, on the south side of it, we follow an enchanted ancient greenway before striking up into stark open moorland, reminiscent of Scotland.

Access by car:
From **Brecon**, take the A40 towards **Carmarthen**, and in the village of **Trecastle** choose the second left turning, signed 'Usk Reservoir' which leads through **Cwmwysg** and along the edge of the reservoir. At a T-junction, turn right and just before leaving the forest, turn left into a small car park.

A longer alternative
Start at Wp.1 of **Usk Reservoir** (Route 38) to join this route at Wp.3 (Route 38's Wp.6), rejoining it at Wp.2 (Route 38's Wp.8) and so add to the variety by initially walking beside the water and finally through the forest; a full day.

From the forest car park (Wp.1 0M) we cross the road and pass though a gate to the left of a green metal barrier to walk down a gravel track (N). Another track goes up to the right between mature conifers (Wp.2 5M)

(N.B. If you're walking the longer alternative, this is your way.)

We go straight on, sweeping to the left (W) past a large gravel space to our right. Following a green cycle waymark we descend to cross a bridge over **Nant Tarw**, then climb through an area where all the trees have been felled and new ones planted.

... glorious views of the Camarthen Fens ...

Looking back, there are glorious views of the **Carmarthen Fans** before we enter mature woodland, the way undulating until we see the reservoir between the trees on our right. Emerging from the woods with the reservoir now close by, we cross a stile in the fence on our left beside a pond (Wp.3 28M) into open moorland.

We're still going in the same general direction (W) but now along a less than obvious path to the left of the valley bottom. Up the other side we can see an obvious path and when opposite (Wp.4 35M) turn right (NW) to make straight for it across tussocky grass. But just after beginning to climb it we find a path on the left (Wp.5 38M) that takes us diagonally (W), slightly up the contour.

The attractive cleft

As we steadily climb, the valley we've traversed deepens to our left with a rocky outcrop and an attractive cleft that runs away from us at right angles from the main valley, towards the mountains. Reaching the bluff, we swing right (NW) and drop gently down to a plantation enclosed by a tumbledown dry stone wall and a fence.

The path runs parallel to the dry stone wall and goes gently down but along a steep slope which makes the going tricky in places. At the end of this boundary a deep gully opens up to our left and we cross the stream that runs in it (Wp.6 62M); here, the main path continues along the contour while we take a minor path to our left which goes steeply down by the gully (W).

After the path becomes grassy and less steep, we reach a fork (Wp.7 66M) and take the left hand option to go gently down a steady decline towards a wooded valley.

The path runs beside the boundary at the top of a field which consists of ancient trees assisted by barbed wire and, after passing a rocky outcrop on our right, goes through a metal barred gate (Wp.8 81M). We continue in the same direction down an old grassy way between hawthorns until swinging right (S) to go steeply down into a gorge beside a tinkling stream.

In the midst of this idyllic landscape we are confronted by double metal gates in a sheepfold unattractively constructed from breeze blocks. What has become a muddy track bends to the right (W) as it meets a river in the valley and crosses 'our' stream.

The map indicates that we should cross the river, but as there isn't a convenient place we follow the farm track through a rusty gate to meet a narrow lane (Wp.9 90M).

Here, we turn left (SW) and can now cross the river to follow the lane as it wanders left and right, up and down until we meet the Roman road (Wp.10 113M). Turning right (W) we march along like legionnaires, in anticipation of refreshment at the pub (Wp.11 121M).

Retracing our steps after lunch to Wp.10 we turn right (S) down a track to the right hand side of a chapel between hedges, ignoring gates to left and right. It becomes muddy and rocky before we pass through a rusty barred gate and go right (SW) and steeply down, swinging to left and right. Over a stile to the right of another metal barred gate, we continue down this ancient greenway between gracious old trees with rocks protruding from banks on both sides. It's just beautiful and when a babbling brook joins us we feel that all is well with the world!

Hearing a larger stream in front of us, we go ever steeper down through this enchanted wood and over a stile to the right of a rusty barred gate with three large steps down its other side, to reach a bridge and cross the stream (Wp.12 140M).

The path goes to the right, the other side of the valley; leaving the wood, we cross a stile to the left of a gate and come up to the left of a house (Wp.13 145M SE). Joining the tarmacked track (the owner's link with the rest of the world) we go through a new metal barred gate and steeply up (SSW).

Meeting the lane at a corner (Wp.14 160M), we turn left and proceed into **Llandeusant**, passing the YHA Hostel on our right. At a T-junction (Wp.15 166M) we turn left again (E) signed 'Llyn y Fan' and after only two minutes fork left (Wp.16 168M NE) to go over a stile and along a footpath between hedges.

After a stile to the left of a metal barred gate we cross a track, the way now a sunken lane between fields, wet in places so that you'll find walking on the right field edge easier. Another stile, this time to the right of a gate, leads us to a sunken lane crossroads (Wp.17 179M) where we turn right (E).

The views ahead of **Fan Foel** and the escarpment that runs above **Llyn y Fan Fach** and **Llyn y Fan Fawr** are truly stunning. Again, it's easier to walk on the field edge in places - not because the lane is wet, but because it's strewn with branches, small bushes and marsh grass - this is confirmed by the next stile's position up on the left field edge. After the next very high stile to the left of a metal barred gate (Wp.18 186M), we are out on open moorland.

Up to our left is **Mynydd y Llan** but we can see our way ahead, a steady climb up a green hollow to the right of it. To our relief, most of the climbing is done, and the way soon flattens out, and it's now downhill (almost) all of the way back.

Fan Foel

The **Sawddle Valley** drops deep down to our right and we can see **Fan Foel** prominent as we stride over the springy turf. Most of our journey back is without event but we do cross a gully (Wp.19 216M) which requires us to climb over rocks to get up out of it and ignore a minor path to the left (Wp.20 228M) which runs up to the top of **Bryn Mawr**. Most importantly, where the paths divide (Wp.21 233M) we take the lower, left hand one (NE) and can soon see, albeit in the distance, the reservoir and its surrounding conifer forest.

We must head towards its left hand end; there are many paths (some made by walkers, others by sheep), but in general terms we head down into the valley of the infant **River Usk** to follow its left hand bank (NNE) back to the car park (Wp.1 284M).

Some might dismiss this route as simply a circuit of the reservoir, while others whose memories are longer might denigrate the area by describing it as 'man made'. Neither would be wrong, but both would miss the point that this leisurely stroll of not much more than two hours can provide a larger dose of that combination of woodland, water and mountain that so uniquely refreshes the soul, than many a longer tramp in a more 'original' environment.

Access by car:
From **Brecon**, we take the A40 towards **Carmarthen**, and in the village of **Trecastle** choose the second left turning, signed 'Usk Reservoir' which leads us through **Cwmwysg**, directly to the car park at the southern end of the dam's reservoir. Park here, looking straight across the reservoir to boats pulled up on the other side.

Crossing the dam

From the car park (Wp.1 0M) we walk across the dam (NW), tarmacked as a road but restricted by padlocked barriers. Pausing to look at the wind-flecked waves, we're not quite able to see the extent of our intended perambulation.

At the other side of the dam we turn left (Wp.2 9M WNW), continuing on tarmac past sailing dinghies on our left and a shed with what looks intriguingly like an orange parking ticket machine inside; poke your noses around the door and you'll discover that it's a machine for issuing fishing permits. Passing an isolated house on our right, we envy the beautiful views that must be enjoyed by its owners across the reservoir to the **Carmarthen Fans**. Looking back, it's surprising to be able to see **Pen y Fan** and **Corn Du** on the horizon, poking up from behind **Fan Frynach** with **Fforest Fach** closer still.

After ignoring a track up to the left, we find cars belonging to lone fishermen parked every hundred metres or so - wonder if they suffer the equivalent of a traffic warden if they fail to purchase a ticket? We pass conifers on the right and a picnic bench left, before we sweep around to the left (SSW) where our easy progress is halted by a locked gate (Wp.3 25M).

... views across the water ...

Our way is over a stile up on our right (SW) and along a delightful bluebell-lined woodland footpath.Leaving the wooded area, the reservoir opens up again on our left; the views across the water are now even more stunning than those from the house.

Sometimes the path takes us to the water's edge and we walk along a stony beach, while now and again there's a choice of beach or a route heading slightly away from the reservoir into woodland - in each case, we choose the woodland. At one point (Wp.4 33M) a grassy bank by the water makes an ideal spot to sit down and bask in the sun.

It seems that we are now beyond the fishermen's areas, as the path is not so well-trodden, though it's still distinct and easy to follow.

View from our elevated position

Our languid progress is interrupted when the path suddenly leaves the reservoir and threads its way up between dark conifers to pop out onto a track, where we turn left and walk through the forest; overall, we continue in the same direction. Although we have only gained a little height, the glimpses we have of the reservoir between the trees take on an entirely different aspect.

Further on, when we emerge from the forest and the grass slopes down to the water, our elevated position allows us to see right along the reservoir to the dam before our track disappears into the forest again.

As we reach the end of the reservoir the track swings left (S) and ahead we can see that it crosses a stream via a ford. You could splash through it, but by turning right into a clearing with a picnic bench, we find an attractive 'Billy Goat Gruff' wooden bridge (Wp.5 71M) that we use as an alternative. Continuing along the track (SE), we spot a stile just after a pond on our right (Wp.6 74M) which leads into open moorland.

(N.B. If you are walking the longer version of **Llandeusant** (Route 37) then this is your way, but begin climbing gently and keep swinging around the end of the reservoir left (SE) passing submerged trees.)

The way undulates through the forest until it swings right (S) away from the reservoir in order to find a crossing place over the **Nant Tarw** which is too large to ford. Wild ponies calmly graze where the forest has been felled and replanted, almost oblivious of us - wonder what the attraction is for them here? The track drops down to meet the river and a substantial bridge (Wp.7 100M).

After climbing steadily up from the river (E) we swing to the right (SE) past a large open area of gravel standing, then gently descend to a junction (Wp.8 107M) where we turn left to steadily climb another gravel track, this time between mature trees. These well-made tracks have obviously been constructed so that timber can be extracted, and they also make good cycle tracks, confirmed by green signs along our route.

Going left, we join another similar track (Wp.9 114M N) then turn right at a T-junction (Wp.10 119M E), mature conifers to our left, newly planted ones right. The way continues to undulate until we come to a green painted metal barrier (Wp.11 126M) where we turn left onto a road (N), fork right by a prominent **Usk Valley** Information Board and return to our car beside the dam (Wp.1 137M).

Unfortunately, there are no hostelries even close to this isolated point, but one suggestion is to carry on along the road that brought us here, turning right at a T-junction to the **Cross Inn** near **Llandeusant** where after refreshment the spectacle of red kites being fed can be enjoyed.

Carn Goch, which roughly translates to 'red rocky hill', is the site of **Y Gaer Fawr** (Wales' largest hill fort), and its sister **Y Gaer Fach**. This route takes us into both of them to look over and beyond the **River Towy**, then up around **Trichrug Hill**, through woods and back down what seems like a long forgotten sunken lane to our start. Some of the way may be overgrown, especially in summer, but making the effort is well worthwhile and will make walking for the next brave soul that much easier. There are no refreshments on the route but **The Red Lion**, one of three pubs in **Llangadog**, should satisfy most tastes.

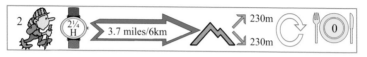

Access by car: from **Brecon**, take the A40 towards **Carmarthen**. After passing through **Llandovery**, turn left onto the A4069 into **Llangadog** and at the village take the right fork that heads right over **The Black Mountain** to **Swansea**. Just outside **Llangadog**, go right again signed 'Bethlehem' and reaching its village sign, turn left into a lane that swings around to the right following signs to 'Garn Goch'. Turning left into a 'No Through Road', park immediately on the left in a grass layby with an information board.

From the information board (Wp.1 0M) we climb straight up (NE) a well-defined path between bracken. The way is steep at first, but we are rewarded with beautiful views over the **River Towy**. As we go higher, and a little around to the right (E), more of the view opens up. We reach a stone wall (Wp.2 8M) which marks the ramparts of **Y Gaer Fach** (Small Fort). Crossing its grassy plateau, views to the right of **Mynydd Myddfai** can be enjoyed.

The mountain of rocks at Wp.3

Passing out of the fort between large piles of rocks, the way is gently down, and there's every chance of seeing a pair of red kites as there's a feeding station behind **The Cross Inn** near **Llandeusant** where they congregate. After a path joins us from the right, we veer right (SE) to approach a mountain of rocks (Wp.3

18M) where we climb left away from the main path (ENE) up into **Y Gaer Fawr** (Big Fort). Again, there's a grassy plateau; we go straight across to an enormous pile of rocks which is the summit (Wp.4 24M), then right down a small path between tussocky grass to rejoin the main path. Why most visitors choose to miss this experience I can't imagine!

The obvious grassy path

We turn left onto the obvious grassy path between bracken which snakes down in front of us towards a wooded ridge with a lane running to the left of it. Turning right (E) to join another path (Wp.5 33M) we pass through a gap in a rock wall which is the fort's lower defence to continue down (SE) to a moorland road (Wp.6 39M).

Turning right again (S), we walk gently uphill. After passing a wooden gate the tarmac disappears, and twenty five metres later (Wp.7 42M) we take a path on the left between hedges, not obvious as even though it's waymarked, it's overgrown. We cross a stile, then it's a new gate on the right and an older one on the left before the path changes into a well-defined track heading steady uphill before it changes again into a sunken lane.

After passing tumbledown farm buildings to our right, the way becomes steeper; take the opportunity to stop to look back across the valley and marvel at the massive iron age constructions. Ahead, we seem to be heading straight up **Trichrug Hill** but the way thankfully veers to the right (SSW) around its shoulder; we go through a wooden barred gate to enter an unusual paddock-like space (Wp.8 60M). Across to the left in the opposite corner, we turn right through another gate to continue upward; the way is still track-width and grassy, but now runs across a field.

Immediately after a new metal barred gate we turn right (Wp.9 71M SW) to squeeze between gorse and the field edge, slipping and sliding on mud to splash through a stream and make for an obvious stile. On the other side we find an out of place shale track that takes us right into a field, where it promptly disappears. Our way is along the top field edge to the far corner (Wp.10 82M) - not as the OS map would have us believe - then through a gap in a dry stone wall and right (W) to travel between dry stone wall to the right and fence to the left over a stile and into woods. Now that we're here, it becomes apparent that there are no trees, only heather and masses of gorse.

Heather and masses of gorse

It's not that well walked, but a waymark confirms our way right (NW) and go steeply down the hill between newly planted trees to find a track and a old wooden barred gate (Wp.11 98M).

After clambering over a high stile we plunge down left, into what seems like an impenetrable jungle, though we find the way goes gently down to the right of a fence, an enchanting no man's land where ancient woodland wilderness meets modern farmland.

Over a stile, the way appears to be a swamp with a stream to its left, so the edge of the field to our right seems like the sensible option. Then a plank bridge (Wp.12 110M) with stiles each side takes us into a field with lots of marsh grass, where our way is not obvious. However, carrying on in the same direction, look out for a waymark and go to the left and down the right hand side of the next field. We cross the stream at its bottom by balancing on stones and a conveniently positioned concrete block, then head slightly to the left towards a gate in the far corner of the next field.

Now we go slightly to the right and down the middle of the next narrow field, a larger stream away to the left, and head to the left of a house, then swing right to meet a lane (Wp.13 122M). Turning right along it (NE) we pass the house with its colourful garden, our lane swinging to the left (NW) and descending gently to a T-junction (Wp.14 132M). Turning right again (NE) signed to 'Bethlehem' we continue downhill and reach yet another right turning where our car waits on the left (Wp.1 135M).

In the far western corner of the **Brecon Beacons National Park** hides this jewel, a romantic dream of a castle dramatically perched on top of a precipitous 100 metre limestone crag, inaccessible except from the north. This route takes us down into the **Cennen Valley** and circles around to give ever changing views of the castle. Exploration of the castle itself is well worth while, particularly the dark, underground passage to a well on the cliff edge which supplied water during the many sieges that marked its history.

Access by car: Take the A40 from **Brecon** towards **Carmarthen**. After passing through **Llandovery**, turn left onto the A4069 into **Llangadog** and at the village take the right fork that heads right over **The Black Mountain** to **Swansea**. After three miles we turn right signed 'Gwynfe' and after passing through the village follow signposts to **Trappe** until the castle is visible across fields to the left. Its car park is reached by turning down a lane back on yourself. At one T-junction, **Trappe** isn't visibly signed but by going left signed 'Brynammam', our route, a matching right, appears around the corner.

From the castle's car park (Wp.1 0M), we pass an information board on our right and go right into a farmyard where tickets are on sale for castle entry (but not needed if just completing the walk), torches can be hired to explore the underground passage and refreshments can be bought.

The gate at Wp.2

Heading towards the castle ruins, we go through a kissing gate to the left of a metal barred gate (Wp.2 4M) and up a concreted pathway by a field edge (SSE). Through another gate following an arrow with a castle sign, the path becomes tarmacked and curves left (SE).

There's a feeling of being corralled between hedge on left and fence on right, no doubt a result of the number of

visiting tourists, though we soon lose them when the tarmac path swings right to take them up to the castle (Wp.3 9M), while we go straight on, following an unusual footpath signpost.

The way is quite steep, down a grassy path with lovely views ahead (E), past a couple of benches that are well placed

... an unusual footpath signpost ...

for admiring the beautiful vista. At the bottom of the hill we resist the temptation of a bridge over the **Afon Cennen** (Wp.4 21M) and a 'Castle Long Walk' signpost, instead heading sharp right to follow the 'Castle Short Walk' signpost along the river bank (WSW); unsurprisingly we'll be keeping to neither of them.

Climbing a little above the river, we cross a stile on our left (Wp.5 26M), then descend steps to the river and the water meadow beside it. With a step up to another stile and the next field, the river is now the other side of a fence, as we carry on to a choice of kissing gate or stile either side of a gate (Wp.6 31M). We sweep around to the left (E) and through another metal barred gate to head up a track that goes over a bridge and up to **Hengrofft Farm**.

Feeling a little intrusive, we enter the farmyard, keeping the house to our right and leaving through another gate. Steadily climbing, we are rewarded with fantastic views of the castle on the top of the cliff behind us before, with a path to our left and a choice of tracks (Wp.7 43M), we fork right, the steepest of the three ways.

... fantastic views of the castle ...

Going more slowly now because this track is steeper, we hairpin to the right (SW) following a signpost with a castle symbol, but where the track hairpins to the left (Wp.8 46M), we go straight on steadily climbing along what becomes a sunken lane between banks of gorse.

The ever-changing view of the castle which still dominates the landscape is now to our right. Approaching the end of the climb out of the valley, a fence is on our right as we go over a high stile to the right of a new metal barred gate, passing more gorse and going through a small metal gate into a field. Now we are forced to walk between fences over the top of the hill (S).

After passing a triangle of trees in the corner of the field, we are presented with a choice of gate or stile (Wp.9 74M) before meeting a track with a house on the left which we join. Following it around to the left (ESE), we then go over a stile to the side of a metal barred gate to a mountain road (Wp.10 78M), then head right (S) and over a cattle grid beside a jumbled dry stone wall and an ivy-encased tree. After passing enormous rocky boulders piled up to our left, the lane bends right (WSW) before we turn right over a stile to the left of a metal barred gate, into a field following a 'Carreg Cennen Circular Walk' signpost (Wp.11 83M). Ahead of us are two fenced off areas that look like bomb craters; they are actually *shake holes*, a geological feature of the area where the underlying limestone causes the land to slip away. Going to the left of both of them (NW) we spot a stile to the right of a rusty barred gate which leads us to a path (WSW) close to a dry stone wall. Our path becomes a track which sweeps down to the right (NW) and then to the left (W) before we become aware of a valley dropping steeply to our left, beyond a sturdy fence. The gurgle of water that's now audible comes from the source of the **River Loughor** which emerges from a cave, though the dire warnings on a notice by a stile on our left discourage our exploration; instead, we continue over a stile to the right of a rusty barred gate and follow the track (WNW) away from the river.

The way becomes a sunken lane, a very wet sunken lane, so we resort to the right hand field edge before crossing some neatly positioned stepping stones and another abnormally high stile (Wp.12 101M). Over the next stile to the right of a metal barred gate we meet a tarmac track with signs for 'Castle Walk' to both left and right.

The castle comes back into view

We go right (E) and down to splash across a ford then left (NNE) and after a cattle grid, the castle comes back into view. A wooden gate bars the way to **Llwyn-bedw Farm** (Wp.13 114M), but we follow the waymark that takes us to the left of it (N), down a faint path across a field, heading towards the left end of the cliff on which the castle is perched.

Crossing a stile, we bear left in the next field to go more steeply down (WNW) to a bridge back over the **Afon Cennen** (Wp.14 119M). It's only slightly uphill to the first stile (N), but more steeply to the second and finally, bearing left, steeper still to the third stile and a lane where we go left (Wp.15 125M W), ascending steadily between hedges. After swinging right (N) the way flattens (a relief, as you're likely to be quite out of puff), and on our right we find a kissing gate to the left of a metal barred gate (Wp.16 130M). This takes us to a path (NE) which crosses a field towards the left of a building which you'll recognize as the castle café. Through a wooden barred gate, the car park is on our left (Wp.1 139M).

See 'Using GPS in the Brecon Beacons on page 19.

1
YSGYRYD FAWR
Wp	Zn	North	East
1	SO	32879	16418
2	SO	32732	16641
3	SO	32737	16885
4	SO	32735	16959
5	SO	32815	17134
6	SO	32824	17262
7	SO	32950	17686
8	SO	33117	18290
9	SO	33068	18075
10	SO	33367	18467
11	SO	33320	18536
12	SO	32924	18438

2
CRIB Y GARTH
Wp	Zn	North	East
1	SO	28855	32860
2	SO	28730	32627
3	SO	27416	33725
4	SO	27329	33971
5	SO	27196	34194
6	SO	27099	34318
7	SO	26526	34954
8	SO	26294	35383
9	SO	27485	34820
10	SO	28023	33802
11	SO	28521	33229

3
HATTERRALL RIDGE
Wp	Zn	North	East
1	SO	28848	32862
2	SO	28783	32492
3	SO	28304	32373
4	SO	28082	32215
5	SO	28007	32050
6	SO	27752	32106
7	SO	27480	32330
8	SO	27045	31967
9	SO	26021	34051
10	SO	25069	36065
11	SO	26299	35382
12	SO	26526	34954
13	SO	27099	34318
14	SO	27416	33725

4
HAY BLUFF
Wp	Zn	North	East
1	SO	23954	37339
2	SO	24285	36484
3	SO	24435	36631
4	SO	23527	35239
5	SO	22484	35064
6	SO	21995	34646
7	SO	22006	35037
8	SO	22121	35659
9	SO	22584	36325

5
CAPEL-Y-FFIN
Wp	Zn	North	East
1	SO	25514	31423
2	SO	25995	31235
3	SO	26396	31020
4	SO	26496	31230
5	SO	26524	31414
6	SO	26707	31702
7	SO	26799	32171
8	SO	26009	34081
9	SO	25066	36068
10	SO	24431	36633
11	SO	23531	35233
12	SO	22485	35065
13	SO	22013	34645
14	SO	23106	33593
15	SO	23446	33220
16	SO	23749	32841
17	SO	24187	32295

6
VALE OF EWYAS
Wp	Zn	North	East
1	SO	25513	31425
2	SO	25817	31026
3	SO	25892	30834
4	SO	26154	30728
5	SO	26533	30333
6	SO	26992	29813
7	SO	27179	29517
8	SO	27217	29017
9	SO	27461	28275
10	SO	27466	28032
11	SO	27707	27908
12	SO	28009	27825
13	SO	28180	27964
14	SO	28704	27866
15	SO	28835	27879
16	SO	28931	28060
17	SO	28858	28496
18	SO	28692	28648
19	SO	28917	29654
20	SO	28105	30773
21	SO	27045	31962
22	SO	26522	31415
23	SO	26498	31226
24	SO	26067	31178

7
BAL MAWR
Wp	Zn	North	East
1	SO	25512	31428
2	SO	25107	31531
3	SO	24947	30908
4	SO	25064	30108
5	SO	25819	29420
6	SO	26762	27097
7	SO	27340	26620
8	SO	27576	26986
9	SO	28136	27332
10	SO	28377	27447
11	SO	28549	27518
12	SO	28738	27688
13	SO	28851	27860
14	SO	28693	27861
15	SO	28180	27965
16	SO	28004	27818
17	SO	27705	27900
18	SO	27453	28040
19	SO	27265	28581
20	SO	27175	29515
21	SO	26637	30201
22	SO	26524	30330
23	SO	26409	30447
24	SO	26215	30633
25	SO	25822	31026

8
CWMYOY
Wp	Zn	North	East
1	SO	29917	23400
2	SO	29889	23533
3	SO	30178	23751
4	SO	30284	23979
5	SO	30583	24597
6	SO	30840	24753
7	SO	31017	24984
8	SO	30834	25826
9	SO	30756	26971
10	SO	29703	27718
11	SO	29396	27858
12	SO	28958	27886
13	SO	28845	27874
14	SO	28766	27607
15	SO	28861	27350
16	SO	28694	27344
17	SO	29063	26910
18	SO	29227	26367
19	SO	29145	25962
20	SO	28604	25116
21	SO	28504	24503
22	SO	28852	23986
23	SO	28949	24279

Wp	Zn	North	East
24	SO	29258	24363
25	SO	29804	23916

9

PONT CADWGAN

Wp	Zn	North	East
1	SO	26718	25130
2	SO	27095	25125
3	SO	27260	25025
4	SO	27925	24537
5	SO	28335	24030
6	SO	28406	24267
7	SO	28663	25192
8	SO	28976	25822
9	SO	29220	26375
10	SO	28693	27345
11	SO	28779	27588
12	SO	28832	27871
13	SO	28358	27435
14	SO	27576	26988
15	SO	27334	26613
16	SO	26853	26258
17	SO	26405	26274
18	SO	26243	26057
19	SO	26838	25931

10

MYNYDD DU

Wp	Zn	North	East
1	SO	26713	25141
2	SO	26833	25913
3	SO	26197	26156
4	SO	25893	26983
5	SO	25000	28982
6	SO	25075	28714
7	SO	24873	28876
8	SO	24763	29126
9	SO	22947	28763
10	SO	23933	27607
11	SO	24220	26720
12	SO	24752	25526
13	SO	25681	24481
14	SO	26019	23715
15	SO	26483	23591
16	SO	26841	23708
17	SO	26962	24313

11

MYNYDD LLANGORSE

Wp	Zn	North	East
1	SO	16070	28332
2	SO	16147	27338
3	SO	15948	26795
4	SO	15722	26109
5	SO	15828	25688
6	SO	15928	25007
7	SO	15312	24985
8	SO	15163	25425
9	SO	14928	25669
10	SO	15030	26215
11	SO	15275	26578
12	SO	15628	27142
13	SO	15810	27648
14	SO	15943	28030

12

LLANGORSE LAKE

Wp	Zn	North	East
1	SO	12909	27392
2	SO	12570	27287
3	SO	12252	26871
4	SO	12102	26534
5	SO	12251	26375
6	SO	12279	26117
7	SO	12374	25972
8	SO	12353	25690
9	SO	12237	25402
10	SO	12346	25198
11	SO	12458	24731
12	SO	12618	24359
13	SO	12877	23717
14	SO	12985	23357
15	SO	14033	22619
16	SO	14911	22036
17	SO	14965	22191
18	SO	15501	23228
19	SO	15930	25005
20	SO	15314	24994
21	SO	15151	25474
22	SO	14931	25672
23	SO	15273	26579
24	SO	14947	26905
25	SO	14978	27078
26	SO	14227	27656
27	SO	13483	27587
28	SO	13129	27325

13

BLORENGE

Wp	Zn	North	East
1	SO	26323	10765
2	SO	26988	11857
3	SO	27713	12230
4	SO	27781	11836
5	SO	27848	11230
6	SO	28277	11376
7	SO	28409	12015
8	SO	28070	12592
9	SO	27915	12545
10	SO	26001	12176
11	SO	25900	11925
12	SO	25635	11505
13	SO	25478	11232
14	SO	25431	11301
15	SO	25463	10974
16	SO	25459	10556

14

SUGAR LOAF FROM LLANGENNY

Wp	Zn	North	East
1	SO	26857	16722
2	SO	26751	17217
3	SO	26703	17365
4	SO	26543	17876
5	SO	27256	18772
6	SO	25986	18968
7	SO	25539	18256
8	SO	25270	17958
9	SO	25107	18203
10	SO	24025	17962
11	SO	23922	17222
12	SO	24103	17210
13	SO	24197	17002
14	SO	24835	17302
15	SO	25458	17503
16	SO	25583	17280
17	SO	25921	16806
18	SO	26581	16883

15

SUGAR LOAF FROM FRO

Wp	Zn	North	East
1	SO	29221	20047
2	SO	29168	20038
3	SO	29282	19828
4	SO	29107	19726
5	SO	28569	19918
6	SO	28502	19697
7	SO	28104	19405
8	SO	27678	18873
9	SO	27229	18785
10	SO	25640	18955
11	SO	25331	19087
12	SO	25084	19166
13	SO	24583	19046
14	SO	24437	19115
15	SO	24830	19661
16	SO	24631	19626
17	SO	24849	19920
18	SO	25458	20149
19	SO	25644	20247
20	SO	26518	20481
21	SO	27470	20574
22	SO	27540	20358
23	SO	27801	20411
24	SO	27880	20378
25	SO	27916	20389
26	SO	28733	20388
27	SO	28700	20255

16

SUGAR LOAF FROM LLWYN DU

Wp	Zn	North	East
1	SO	28887	16641
2	SO	28739	16473
3	SO	28678	16439
4	SO	27710	17935
5	SO	27646	18190
6	SO	27334	18702
7	SO	27253	18773
8	SO	27537	18797
9	SO	27618	18745
10	SO	28252	18869

Wp	Zn	North	East
11	SO	28689	18720
12	SO	29295	17429
13	SO	29319	17283
14	SO	29215	16604
15	SO	28949	17010
16	SO	28834	17005
17			

BRYN ARW

Wp	Zn	North	East
1	SO	29228	20042
2	SO	29358	19980
3	SO	29318	20192
4	SO	29215	20383
5	SO	29205	20593
6	SO	29140	20777
7	SO	29500	20980
8	SO	29543	20759
9	SO	29729	20745
10	SO	30287	20294
11	SO	30693	20006
12	SO	30740	19595
13	SO	30272	18922
14	SO	30256	18716
15	SO	30610	18580
16	SO	30216	17926
17	SO	30218	17772
18	SO	30032	17671
19	SO	30038	17156
20	SO	29949	16996
21	SO	29701	17156
22	SO	29250	18003
23	SO	28940	18528
24	SO	28288	18898
25	SO	28574	19916
18			

TABLE MOUNTAIN

Wp	Zn	North	East
1	SO	21840	18396
2	SO	2147	18361
3	SO	22331	19262
4	SO	22341	19633
5	SO	22460	19627
6	SO	22383	20089
7	SO	22382	20297
8	SO	22495	20314
9	SO	22735	20593
10	SO	22539	20699
11	SO	22517	20827
12	SO	22297	21065
13	SO	21822	20896
14	SO	22014	20538
15	SO	21949	20105
16	SO	21908	19715
17	SO	21672	19226
18	SO	21429	19069
19			

GRWYNNE FAWR

Wp	Zn	North	East
1	SO	23431	20286
2	SO	23408	20741
3	SO	22866	20752
4	SO	22541	20698
5	SO	22300	21564
6	SO	21705	22373
7	SO	21195	22896
8	SO	20690	24337
9	SO	21299	26071
10	SO	20645	28048
11	SO	20444	28616
12	SO	21633	27503
13	SO	21867	26695
14	SO	22025	25790
15	SO	22620	24858
16	SO	22922	24348
17	SO	23303	23553
18	SO	23495	23009
19	SO	23444	22888
20	SO	23587	22305
21	SO	23451	21227
20			

WAUN FACH

Wp	Zn	North	East
1	SO	17383	29683
2	SO	17388	29716
3	SO	17741	30018
4	SO	17891	30163
5	SO	17990	30318
6	SO	18397	30560
7	SO	18689	30809
8	SO	19259	31026
9	SO	19477	31047
10	SO	20672	31408
11	SO	20723	31256
12	SO	21540	29981
13	SO	20625	29629
14	SO	20445	28637
15	SO	19193	29001
16	SO	18653	28928
17	SO	18030	29146
21			

LLANGATTOCK

Wp	Zn	North	East
1	SO	21035	17834
2	SO	20713	17783
3	SO	20678	17274
4	SO	20560	17204
5	SO	20202	17236
6	SO	18843	17383
7	SO	18707	17447
8	SO	18723	17268
9	SO	18530	16911
10	SO	18600	16803
11	SO	18551	16639
12	SO	19350	15898
13	SO	19444	16028
14	SO	20108	16143
15	SO	20218	16583
16	SO	20265	16650
17	SO	20602	16929
18	SO	21057	17703
22			

LLANGYNIDR

Wp	Zn	North	East
1	SO	14656	20004
2	SO	14424	19805
3	SO	14184	19495
4	SO	13481	19369
5	SO	12895	19381
6	SO	11458	19491
7	SO	11182	20246
8	SO	11332	20497
9	SO	11379	20446
10	SO	12085	20499
11	SO	12580	20133
12	SO	12754	20064
13	SO	13489	19820
23			

TALYBONT-ON-USK

Wp	Zn	North	East
1	SO	11447	22550
2	SO	11078	22173
3	SO	10871	21732
4	SO	10887	21241
5	SO	10900	20258
6	SO	11334	20535
7	SO	11377	20450
8	SO	12079	20500
9	SO	12577	20133
10	SO	12745	20062
11	SO	12425	21434
12	SO	11798	22343
24			

FAN FAWR

Wp	Zn	North	East
1	SN	98179	20332
2	SN	97735	21416
3	SN	97652	22207
4	SN	97552	22124
5	SN	97228	22124
6	SN	96925	22133
7	SN	96663	22724
8	SN	96697	23668
9	SN	96254	23112
10	SN	95973	22668
11	SN	95792	22792
12	SN	96071	21888
13	SN	96169	21738
14	SN	97207	20184
15	SN	97571	19686
16	SN	96991	19353
25			

PEN Y FAN FROM CWM LLWCH

Wp	Zn	North	East
1	SO	00651	24477
2	SO	00442	24108
3	SO	00540	23806

Wp	Zn	North	East
4	SO	00537	23559
5	SO	00389	22885
6	SO	00278	22416
7	SN	99997	22056
8	SO	00074	21778
9	SO	00715	21339
10	SO	01206	21584
11	SO	01964	23268
12	SO	02105	24408
13	SO	02190	24588
14	SO	02382	24733
15	SO	02567	25134
16	SO	02011	25255
17	SO	01226	25199

26

PEN Y FAN FROM TAF FECHAN

Wp	Zn	North	East
1	SO	03534	17370
2	SO	03153	17974
3	SO	02887	17997
4	SO	02179	17733
5	SO	01917	18280
6	SO	00530	20780
7	SO	00614	20980
8	SO	00718	21330
9	SO	01208	21584
10	SO	01780	21209
11	SO	02393	21319
12	SO	03154	20537
13	SO	03364	18189

27

PEN Y FAN FROM PONT AR DAF

Wp	Zn	North	East
1	SN	98762	19882
2	SO	00608	20977
3	SO	00722	21346
4	SO	01207	21598
5	SO	00072	21772
6	SN	99780	22120
7	SN	98828	21837
8	SN	98220	20345

28

FAN Y BIG

Wp	Zn	North	East
1	SO	05620	25519
2	SO	05705	25490
3	SO	05695	25327
4	SO	05661	25050
5	SO	05788	24814
6	SO	05775	24054
7	SO	04705	23006
8	SO	04327	22099
9	SO	03653	20661
10	SO	03168	20536
11	SO	03431	23050
12	SO	03644	23541
13	SO	03798	23736
14	SO	04130	23911
15	SO	04528	24296
16	SO	04701	24744
17	SO	04809	25086

29

LLANFRYNACH

Wp	Zn	North	East
1	SO	07465	25775
2	SO	07553	25530
3	SO	07145	24982
4	SO	07484	24564
5	SO	07446	24245
6	SO	07364	24048
7	SO	07270	23893
8	SO	06674	22516
9	SO	05748	20581
10	SO	05486	20372
11	SO	04464	19660
12	SO	03744	19891
13	SO	03653	20670
14	SO	04310	22035
15	SO	04579	22503
16	SO	05462	23801
17	SO	05634	23937
18	SO	05771	24059
19	SO	05685	24328
20	SO	05971	24558
21	SO	06262	24668
22	SO	06666	25019
23	SO	07188	25777

30

TALYBONT RESERVOIR

Wp	Zn	North	East
1	SO	10531	21002
2	SO	10472	21157
3	SO	0265	20858
4	SO	10094	20673
5	SO	09684	20592
6	SO	09119	20513
7	SO	08769	20539
8	SO	06991	20142
9	SO	05882	20452
10	SO	05808	20490
11	SO	05030	19202
12	SO	05437	18290
13	SO	05610	17597
14	SO	05501	17442
15	SO	07254	16462
16	SO	09194	17246
17	SO	10224	18391
18	SO	10365	19104
19	SO	10459	19664
20	SO	10699	20344
21	SO	10345	20550

31

PONTSTICILL RESERVOIR

Wp	Zn	North	East
1	SO	05499	14340
2	SO	05489	14218
3	SO	04585	13915
4	SO	05662	12034
5	SO	05747	11570
6	SO	06078	11900
7	SO	06235	11897
8	SO	06061	11430
9	SO	06586	11955
10	SO	06670	12531
11	SO	06816	13038
12	SO	06876	13149
13	SO	06064	13207
14	SO	05792	13378
15	SO	05783	13564
16	SO	05836	14440

32

TAF FAWR

Wp	Zn	North	East
1	SO	01334	11392
2	SO	01246	11474
3	SO	00912	11267
4	SO	00791	11350
5	SO	00414	11995
6	SO	00379	12947
7	SO	00483	13190
8	SO	00347	13066
9	SO	00245	13451
10	SO	00228	14301
11	SN	99988	14341
12	SN	99009	16641
13	SN	98964	17443
14	SN	98828	18080
15	SN	98442	18450
16	SN	98374	18771
17	SN	98198	20144
18	SN	98228	20296

33

WATERFALLS

Wp	Zn	North	East
1	SN	91874	10574
2	SN	92244	10793
3	SN	92450	11117
4	SN	92501	10946
5	SN	92349	10594
6	SN	92523	10253
7	SN	92775	10078
8	SN	92804	09984
9	SN	92901	09895
10	SN	92448	09066
11	SN	92242	08370
12	SN	91851	08195
13	SN	91643	08093
14	SN	91097	07939
15	SN	90077	07630
16	SN	90012	07808
17	SN	89895	08413
18	SN	89834	09140
19	SN	89628	09289
20	SN	90256	09678
21	SN	90760	10468

Wp	Zn	North	East
22	SN	91225	10555
23	SN	91251	10744
24	SN	91654	11007
25	SN	91811	10943

34

SGWYD YR EIRA

Wp	Zn	North	East
1	SN	92800	12411
2	SN	92778	12358
3	SN	92465	11138
4	SN	92506	10955
5	SN	92409	10576
6	SN	92556	10180
7	SN	92283	10344
8	SN	92756	10088
9	SN	92884	09991
10	SN	92832	10108
11	SN	92789	10257
12	SN	93387	11073
13	SN	93187	11688
14	SN	93000	12088
15	SN	92827	12175

35

LLYN Y FAN FAWR

Wp	Zn	North	East
1	SN	84882	17148
2	SN	84917	17372
3	SN	84321	17802
4	SN	83384	19420
5	SN	82894	21368
6	SN	83452	21447
7	SN	84044	20947
8	SN	84341	20752
9	SN	84995	20484
10	SN	84981	19692
11	SN	84925	19346
12	SN	85100	19379
13	SN	84993	17233

36

HENRHYD FALLS

Wp	Zn	North	East
1	SN	85308	12090
2	SN	85112	12410
3	SN	84717	12912
4	SN	84566	13669
5	SN	84767	14518
6	SN	84812	14710
7	SN	84650	15181
8	SN	84316	15729
9	SN	83969	15540
10	SN	84144	15183
11	SN	83823	15149
12	SN	83840	14986
13	SN	83012	14262
14	SN	82841	14195
15	SN	82474	13933
16	SN	82332	13555
17	SN	82068	13197
18	SN	81706	12650
19	SN	82470	12875
20	SN	82508	12780
21	SN	82830	12610
22	SN	83071	12534
23	SN	83482	12630
24	SN	83569	12381
25	SN	84820	12005
26	SN	85190	11903
27	SN	85370	11931

37

LLANDDEUSANT

Wp	Zn	North	East
1	SN	82003	27140
2	SN	82027	27422
3	SN	80594	27843
4	SN	80269	27741
5	SN	80188	27836
6	SN	79465	28354
7	SN	79398	28236
8	SN	78696	28076
9	SN	78408	27863
10	SN	77851	26096
11	SN	77297	25872
12	SN	77880	25578
13	SN	77865	25391
14	SN	77782	24877
15	SN	77731	24529
16	SN	77863	24574
17	SN	78256	24861
18	SN	78506	24820
19	SN	79607	24790
20	SN	80238	24614
21	SN	80504	24674

38

USK RESERVOIR

Wp	Zn	North	East
1	SN	83294	28626
2	SN	83174	29077
3	SN	82427	29167
4	SN	81739	28726
5	SN	80545	27955
6	SN	80592	27844
7	SN	81790	27523
8	SN	82028	27429
9	SN	82415	27654
10	SN	82351	27896
11	SN	82774	28019

39

CARN GOCH

Wp	Zn	North	East
1	SN	68151	24234
2	SN	68471	24292
3	SN	68814	24176
4	SN	69011	24291
5	SN	69426	24476
6	SN	69639	24243
7	SN	69596	24060
8	SN	69589	23383
9	SN	69466	22929
10	SN	69291	22757
11	SN	68852	22804
12	SN	68577	23088
13	SN	68154	23455
14	SN	68015	24032

40

CARREG CENNEN CASTLE

Wp	Zn	North	East
1	SN	66668	19343
2	SN	66736	19248
3	SN	66903	19165
4	SN	67508	19277
5	SN	67261	19149
6	SN	67079	19018
7	SN	67708	18982
8	SN	67666	18908
9	SN	67221	18236
10	SN	67370	18019
11	SN	67161	17742
12	SN	66500	18071
13	SN	66702	18446
14	SN	66601	18722
15	SN	66599	18874
16	SN	66514	19093

GLOSSARY

col	depression in a mountain chain
cwm	valley that ends in a bowl shape as its highest extremity
shake holes	geographical feature, particular to the Brecon Beacons, where the underlying limestone has collapsed

APPENDICES

APPENDIX A
WELSH PLACE NAMES

Welsh place names are highly descriptive so we've included the English translations of some words here for you to discover their meanings yourselves. We particularly like the evocative **Llyn y Fan Fach**. 'Welsh Place-names and Their Meanings' by Dewi Davies, available from Tourist Information Offices, is a rich source for further exploration.

aber	river mouth	*du*	black	*nant*	stream
afon	river	*esgair*	mountain	*ogof*	cave
allt	hill, slope		ridge	*pant*	valley
bach	small	*eira*	snow	*pen*	top, head
blaen	source of river	*fan*	peak	*pont*	bridge
bryn	hill	*fach*	nook	*rhiw*	hillside
bwlch	pass	*gaer*	fort	*sgwd*	
cae	field	*graig*	rock, crag	*(scwd)*	waterfall
castell	castle	*heol*	road	*tre*	homestead,
carn	cairn	*llan*	church		town
cefn	ridge	*llech*	flat stone	*twyn*	mound
craig	rock, crag	*llwyn*	bush, grove	*waun*	moorland
crib	crest	*llyn*	lake	*uchaf*	upper, highest
cwm	bowl shaped valley	*mawr*	large	*y, yr*	the
		mynydd	mountain		

APPENDIX B
PUBLIC TRANSPORT

Unsurprisingly for such a lightly populated area, not all the walks described in this book can be accessed by public transport. But the following can:-

1	Ysgyryd Fawr	LA1 from **Abergavenny**
*4	Hay Bluff	B7 from **Hay-on-Wye**
*5	Capel-y-ffin	B7 from **Hay-on-Wye**
*6	Vale of Ewyas	B7 from **Hay-on-Wye**
*7	Bal Mawr	B7 from **Hay-on-Wye**
11	Mynydd Llangorse	RM109 from **Brecon**
12	Llangorse Lake	RM109 from **Brecon**
18	Table Mountain	X43 from **Abergavenny**, **Brecon** or **Merthyr Tydfil**
*22	Llangynidr	B4 from **Newport**, **Abergavenny** or **Brecon**
23	Talybont-on-Usk	X43 from **Abergavenny**, **Brecon** or **Merthyr Tydfil**
24	Fan Fawr	X43 from **Abergavenny**, **Brecon** or **Merthyr Tydfil**

27 Pen y Fan	X43 from **Abergavenny**, **Brecon** or **Merthyr Tydfil**
29 Llanfrynach	X43 from **Abergavenny**, **Brecon** or **Merthyr Tydfil**
30 Talybont Reservoir	X43 from **Abergavenny**, **Brecon** or **Merthyr Tydfil**
31 Pontsticill Reservoir	24 from **Merthyr Tydfil** to **Pontsticill** and start from Wp.5
32 Taf Fawr	X43 from **Abergavenny**, **Brecon** or **Merthyr Tydfil**
33 Waterfalls	161 from **Neath** to **Pontneddfechan** and start from Wp.15
35 Llyn y Fan Fawr	63 from **Brecon** and **Neath**

* accessed by the Beacons Bus only, which at the time of writing only runs on Sundays and Bank Holidays in June, July and August. For further details ask for a leaflet at a Tourist Information Office, ring 01873 853254 or www.visitbreconbeacons.com

For times of the other services, visit the excellent www.travelinecymru.org.uk website or ask at a Tourist Information Office.

APPENDIX C
WHERE TO STAY

For a wide choice of accommodation visit www.visitbreconbeacons.com but, for what it's worth, I've personal experience of the following and am happy to recommend them.

The Crown, Old Hereford Road, Pantygelli, **Abergavenny** NP7 7HR
01873 853314   www.thecrownatpantygelli.com
An upmarket pub bed and breakfast with good food in a quiet village close to **Abergavenny** and convenient for routes 9,10,15 and 17.

Capel-y-ffin Youth Hostel, Llanthony, nr **Abergavenny** NP7 7NP
0870 7705748   www.yha.org.uk
You may be surprised that couples and families now stay in separate rooms rather than dormitories and you don't even need to be a member let alone satisfy the youth tag. This ex-hill farm is *the* place to use as a base for routes 4,5,6 and 7.

The Bear Hotel, High Street, Crickhowell, **Powys**
01873 810408   www.bearhotel.co.uk
Crickhowell would be my choice if you're looking for a town to stay in while exploring the area.   **The Bear** is a fifteenth century coaching inn serving exceptionally good food with routes 18 and 19 starting within easy striking distance.

Grawen Caravan and Camping Park, Cwm Taff, **Merthyr Tydfil**
01685 723740   www.walescaravanandcamping.com
My sort of camp site, being relaxed, friendly and in a beautiful location while still having good showers, hook ups etc. It's easy to access just off the A470 between **Merthyr** and **Brecon** and central for exploring all of the National Park and particularly convenient for routes 24,27 and 32.

Nant-Ddu Lodge Hotel, Cwm Taf, **Merthyr Tydfil**
01685 379111   www.nant-ddu-lodge.co.uk
Just up the road but at the other end of the price spectrum from Grawen, **Nant-Ddu**

has a magnificent position, a pool and a health spa; the food is pretty good too!

Penybryn House, Llangorse, **Brecon**
01874 658606

A homely bed and breakfast with good facilities close to routes 11 and 12. If, like me, you don't like to get back in the car to find somewhere to eat after a day's walking, The Red Lion in the village serves reasonable pub food.

Mandinam, Llangadog, Carmarthenshire SA19 9LA
01550 777368   www.mandinam.co.uk

Half way between bed and breakfast and self catering accommodation, you'll stay in one of two self contained converted outbuildings but be served breakfast in the magnificent dining room of the farmhouse. Convenient for routes 37,38,39 and 40.

Dderi Farm, Glyntawe, Abercrave, **Swansea** SA9 1GT
01639 730458   www.dderifarm.co.uk

A traditional farmhouse bed and breakfast providing direct access to otherwise out of the way route 35. Route 36 is also close. The isolated **Tafarn-y-Garreg** inn is within walking distance.

INDEX OF PLACE NAMES